STAR SIGNS

LORI REID

Cover illustration by
David Scutt

SCHOLASTIC INC.

New York Toronto London Auckland Sydney

ISBN 0-590-21688-0

Text copyright © 1996 by Lori Reid.
Cover illustration copyright © 1996 by David Scutt.
Interior illustrations copyright © 1996 by Scholastic Ltd.
All rights reserved. Published by Scholastic Inc., 555 Broadway, New York, NY 10012, by arrangement with Scholastic Ltd.

SCHOLASTIC and associated logos are trademarks and/or registered trademarks of Scholastic Inc.

12 11 10 9 8 7 6 5 4 3 2   8 9/9 0 1 2 3/0

Printed in the U.S.A.   40
First Scholastic printing, January 1998

Contents

Introduction

What are you like? No, not what do you look like. I mean, what are you really like – fundamentally, deep down inside? Would you find it easy to list your ten best characteristics or, for that matter, your five worst ones?

And what wouldn't you give to see yourself as others see you? To find out exactly how you come across to other people, what they truly think about you, what they like most about you and what they like least?

Well, that's precisely what this book is going to help you find out. It's going to hold up a mirror, if you like, that will reflect back a picture of you.

You've probably read your "stars" in newspapers and magazines, so you'll already know a bit about horoscopes. You'll know, for example, that there are twelve signs of the Zodiac, that each sign occurs at a particular month and that each has its own set of characteristics which describes people born at that time of the year. And, of course, you'll also know what your own sign is.

When you say you're a Libran or a Sagittarian, for example, it's a short-hand way of describing yourself. That's where the mirror comes in, because your Sun sign reflects information about you. All sorts of information – both good and bad, complimentary or otherwise. But it's important information because it's stuff that you can use as a valuable guide throughout your life.

You see, by reading about your birth sign, you can discover your best qualities, your hidden talents, what you like and dislike, what you're good at, how you think and feel, how you behave and relate, what sort of friends you prefer and the kind of relationships you're likely to make.

That's more than enough for starters but, of course, every good astrologer would tell you that Sun signs don't have all the information. If you really wanted the absolute low-down, the whole shebang, every last nitty-gritty detail, you would need to have a proper birth chart drawn up, which would show all the planets in their places at the very moment you were born. It's the unique relationship between the positions of these planets that can give you the whole picture about yourself.

Nevertheless, you can still get a good deal out of your Sun sign and especially so if you combine it with your Moon sign. That's because the position of the Moon at the time you were born will tell you more about your emotions than any other planet in the solarscope. (By the way, technically, the Moon is a "satellite" of earth, but in astrology it's treated as a planet.)

Though you know from your date of birth which sign of the Zodiac you belong to, it's a little trickier to know exactly where the Moon was at that time. But you can find out by turning to the Moon chapter on page 187, which will help you work it out. Then you can read about how the Moon directly affects you personally, and how it combines with your Sun sign, giving you a deeper understanding of your feelings and the way you relate to others.

Of course, there are other factors that influence our lives – our culture and nationality, where we live, what our family is like. And talking about families, if you want to get some inside info on what makes your mom and dad tick, check out Your Star Sign Parents on page 175. This section not only explains how well you get on with your folks, but it also gives you some pretty hot tips on how to get around them with the minimum pain and the maximum gain!

All in all, Star Signs promises to reveal a tremendous amount about you, your life and your loves – from your secret ambition to your ideal partner, from your favorite hobbies to your favorite date, from what your mom thinks about you to your relationships with the opposite sex.

Interested? Then read on – and have fun!

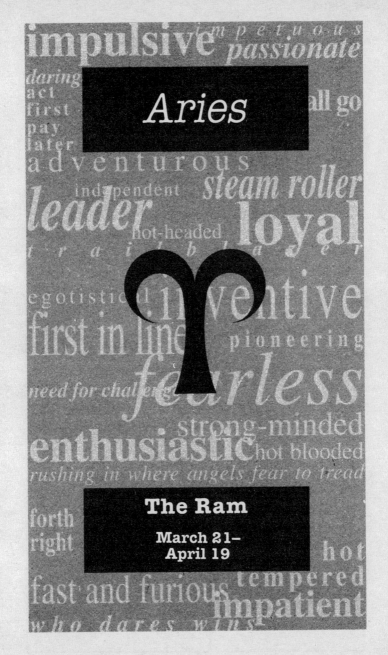

impulsive *impetuous*
passionate

daring
act
first *all go*
pay
later

adventurous

independent *steam roller*

leader loyal
hot-headed
trailblazer

egotistical inventive

first in line pioneering

fearless

need for challenge

strong-minded
enthusiastic hot blooded
rushing in where angels fear to tread

forth
right

The Ram

March 21–
April 19

hot
tempered
fast and furious impatient
who dares wins

Are You A True Aries?

Find out how typical you are of your sign. Check only **one** box for each question.

2   1   0

	Often	Sometimes	Never
Do you do things on impulse?	○	◉	○
Does repetitive work bore you ?	✗	◉	○
Do you take charge of situations?	○	◉	○
How often do you play sport?	◉	○	○
Do you find yourself finishing off people's sentences when you're talking to them?	○	◉	○
Do you get impatient?	◉	○	○
Do you go out of your way to find things that will challenge you?	○	○	◉
Do your mates push you forward when the teacher asks the class to choose a spokes-person?	○	○	◉

	Often	Sometimes	Never
Do you like to go exploring?	○	◉	○
Do you give the impression of being tough and fearless?	○	○	◉
Do you get bored if you're in one place for too long?	◉	○	○
Do you hate it when people tell you what to do?	◉	○	○

Score: You score 2 points for an "Often" answer, 1 point for a "Sometimes" answer, 0 points for a "Never."

0 - 12 You're not a typical Aries, so perhaps you were born at the very beginning or at the very end of your sign, which would modify your character. If so, you're what is known as "cuspal" and are a mixture of two signs. If you were born at the very beginning of Aries, you share some Piscean characteristics and should read about that sign as well. If you were born at the end, you share some Taurean characteristics, so read up on that sign too.

13 - 18 Although you do have many Aries characteristics, your Moon placement probably modifies your character and personality quite noticeably. Find out more by reading about how the Moon affects your emotions on page 18.

19 and Over You're a true Aries. Now read on and find out more about yourself.

Sign Associations

- **Element** – Fire
- **Lucky day** – Tuesday
- **Lucky number** – 1
- **Stone** – Diamond
- **Flower** – Red rose, gladioli
- **Color** – Scarlet
- **Aries rules** – The head and face

Your Ruling Planet

As an Aries, your ruling planet is Mars so you may be interested in some of the things associated with that planet. The symbol for Mars is:

Mars is associated with:

- *energy and drive*
- *courage and a fighting spirit*
- *a love of adventure, exploration, anything new*
- *an aptitude for sports*
- *mechanical ability*
- *interest in combat and military matters*

★ **Famous people who share your sign** ★

Elton John, Linford Christie, Nicholas Lyndhurst, Damon Albarn, Eddie Murphy, Cathy Dennis, Phillip Schofield, Michaela Strachen, Chris Evans, Sean Maguire, Shannon Doherty, Robert Downey Jr.

Keynotes to Aries

you belong to the fire element, so: you're enthusiastic, warm, open, generous and friendly. You're noisy and extroverted.

your talents and interests lie in: sports and games. Fashion design. The martial arts. Engineering. Motor mechanics. Debating. Invention, construction and innovation. Daring exploits.

you work: enthusiastically and energetically for as long as your interest lasts. But you're ace at finding as many short-cuts as you can.

you hate: hitches and hold-ups.

at school: you're always in a rush on school mornings because you want to get there before the bell rings, so you can have time with your friends before classes begin. When the whistle blows, you'll rush to be first in line. In fact, you rush all over the place and often get scolded for running in the halls. The worst bit about school is doing boring exercises over and over again. The best bit is sports. You're a champ on a sport's field. Because you're tough, you respect people who are strong but you get a tad impatient with weaker kids, and you have to be careful that they don't see you as a bit of a bully. Whether or not you were first to arrive, when you hear that last bell you'll get your gear on quickly and make sure you're the first to leave.

you spend your money: on the best trainers you can buy. On accessories for your racing bike.

you like your bedroom to be: there when you

need it! You're usually in such a hurry that it often looks as if a tornado's hit it! But you have an effective method for cleaning up when your mom tells you to – you just kick all the mess under the bed. Otherwise, you cultivate the cluttered look. You like your room to reflect your fiery personality so you'll probably have lots of dramatic red and black paintwork or accessories and, of course, your sporting trophies will be everywhere.

*you keep **fit** by:* doing everything *fast*. By becoming the county's junior cross-country champ. Or by being the school sport's champion, ace swimmer or judo superstar.

♈ ♈ ♈

The Aries Personality

Because Aries is the first sign of the Zodiac, people born under this sign find that taking the lead, heading the pack, and being first is stamped into their character. Being at the top of the pecking order will inevitably influence their behavior and the things that they do. Throughout their lives, circumstances just seem to push them to the front every time.

For a start, they're quick. Everything they do, they do at the speed of light. They simply can't slow down – they don't know how to! They have to rush in order to finish first or to get there before anyone else does. That's why so many Aries folk become explorers, discoverers, inventors and pioneers.

These people are human dynamos. They're born with an amazing amount of energy. And it's on the sports field that they can show what they're really made of. Sports challenge them and give them the chance to run faster, swim further, throw longer, climb higher. They can win games, they can break records – and many of them have gotten the trophies (not to mention the T-shirts) to prove it!

Theirs is a mega personality – even without that habit of showing off a teensy-weensy little bit! Just think how dull any gathering would be without their noisy boisterousness, their lively, incessant chatter or their audacious daredevilry. Parties simply wouldn't be parties without them.

If you're an Aries, do you think you're anything like this picture of the Rambo Ram or Effervescent Ewe?

What you really think about yourself but wouldn't dream of saying to anyone else: *I'm a winner.*

What you want most in the world: *To do it first.*

What your mom would say to you: *Are you turbocharged or something? Just slow down, will you, I can't keep up with you!*

What your teacher would write in your school report: *Never afraid to try.*

What your best friend would say to you: *I wish I had your guts.*

How to insult an Aries: *Back off, you pushy pipsqueak, and get to the back of the line where you belong!*

If your boyfriend is a typical Aries...

You can spot him a mile away because he's: got a broad forehead, bushy eyebrows, close-set eyes, a long nose and a small chin. If you remember, Aries is the sign of the Ram and in fact, looking at him side-ways on, his profile does rather remind you of a sheep! Now, check out his feet. Are they tiny? Well, that just about confirms it then. Other than that, your Aries boy loves wearing smart, trendy clothes and he'd look particularly gorgeous in a uniform.

- **He likes:** *anything new – and he has to have it before any other kid on the block.*

- **He needs:** *a challenge.*

- **He's great because he's:** *direct.*

- **He's a drag because he's:** *all elbows!*

- **Never:** *push in front of him.*

On your first date with him: expect an exhausting but thrilling few hours ahead. This guy's a goer and he literally won't keep still. If you can't stand the pace he's probably not the right guy for you. He likes taking charge, so like it or not he'll have planned everything without even asking you what you want to do. He might take you swimming or to a club. He might challenge you to a game of tennis or suddenly produce a couple of tickets to go and see a football game. This guy falls in love at first sight and doesn't waste any time before moving in. He's pushy by nature so be prepared for him to come on strong.

On his birthday, spoil him: by taking him to a fast-paced all-action movie.

If your girlfriend is a typical Aries...

You can spot her a mile away because she's: got thick, curly, fleece-like hair. She's strikingly attractive, with a longish face and distinctively high cheekbones. She comes across like a cheerleader: strong, vital and athletic-looking with a face that radiates health and fitness. She likes being trendy but needs to be comfortable as well. She hates anything tight or clothes that restrict her movements in any way. So, she'll more than likely be wearing jeans or leggings or perhaps a track suit in her favorite shade of red.

- **She likes:** *partying.*

- **She needs:** *variety.*

- **She's great because she's:** *honest.*

- **She's a drag because she's:** *selfish.*

- **Never:** *dampen her enthusiasm.*

On your first date with her: you'd better check what she wants to do first – Aries girls don't like being ordered around. If you want to make a good impression, use your imagination. She likes doing things on the spur of the moment, so dream up something exciting that will take her breath away. If the fair's in town, take her on the ferris wheel or, even better, on the roller coaster. Ride the bumper cars, challenge her to a shoot-out on the rifle range, grab a hot dog, share cotton candy, swap jokes. This is one girl who won't let any guy get the best of her. She's sure to give as good as she gets!

On her birthday, spoil her: by treating her to a session at the local ski slope.

Aries in love

♥ **You have a special understanding with:** Leos, Sagittarians and, of course, other Aries.

♥ **In a relationship your best qualities are:** staunch loyalty, generosity, true affection, sense of fun.

♥ **In a relationship your worst qualities are:** selfishness, bossiness, losing interest the moment you can't get your own way.

♥ **Your ideal partner:** is someone who is strong but not bossy, loving but not too clingy. It must be someone who is energetic and outgoing yet prepared to let you take the lead. But, because you can get restless and because you like to do the chasing, in order to keep your attention, this partner will definitely have to give you a good run for your money!

Dos & don'ts for happy relationships

do ✓	don't ✗
✓ remember to share	✗ come on too strong, too soon
✓ something funny, spontaneous or impulsive occasionally to surprise your partner	✗ jump to conclusions and run off with someone else the minute something goes wrong

Your Aries love chart

Aries with ♥	Your relationship together	♥ At a glance
Aries	great buddies, great passion	♥♥♥♥♥
Taurus	yes! yes! yes!	♥♥♥
Gemini	good friends, good fun	♥♥♥♥
Cancer	not on the same wave-length	♥
Leo	sizzling	♥♥♥♥♥
Virgo	a bit of a slow starter	♥♥
Libra	attraction of opposites?	♥♥♥
Scorpio	wow!	♥♥♥♥
Sagittarius	racy, pacy and fun, fun, fun	♥♥♥♥♥
Capricorn	a scorcher if you give it time	♥♥♥♥
Aquarius	hmm! interesting	♥♥
Pisces	in your dreams	♥

♥ = grim   ♥♥ = so-so   ♥♥♥ = stick with it

♥♥♥♥ = magnetic   ♥♥♥♥♥ = fwoarrrgh!

The Moon and Your Emotions

Everything you've read about yourself so far has been based on the Sun's position at the time of your birth which, in your case, was in the sign of Aries. This tells you a great deal about your character. But if you want to know more about your emotions, you need to know in which sign the Moon was placed when you were born.

Find your Moon sign by turning to the tables on page 187 then read below how it works with your Sun sign to affect and modify your Aries nature.

Sun in Aries with Moon in:

Aries Being born with the Sun in Aries means that you're energetic and outgoing, enthusiastic and impulsive. Well, with the Moon also in this sign, all those qualities will be multiplied by a factor of ten! This combination makes you unstoppable.

Taurus You're torn between the love of adventure and the need for security. One minute you're drawn to excitement and the next you yearn for a comfy bed and a nice steady routine. Get the balance right and you could have the best of both worlds.

Gemini You rush around all over the place, taking as many short-cuts as you can and leaving a trail of half-finished projects in your wake. The problem is boredom. Your attention jumps all over the place, but you are adaptable and can turn your mind to a wide variety of interests.

Cancer The Moon in Cancer gives you sensitivity, and that can only be to the good since this commodity is in

somewhat short supply among many Ariens. But you work
hard to hide this soft center!

Leo What a hyperactive ball of fire you are! You're a
tornado, a streak of lightning, a hurricane. You move so
fast you leave others standing. You could be a champion
athlete or an actor – but whatever you do you'll always be
in the limelight.

Virgo With the Moon in Virgo a lot of the Aries
fieriness is toned down. Emotionally, you tend to be
calmer than most other Aries and, surprisingly, rather shy
at times too. But you'll still have plenty of spirit, even if
you do worry about the consequences.

Libra Your Arien Sun likes a rough and tumble but your
Libran Moon will insist on order and refinement. One
minute your room looks like a mess and the next you
won't find a sock out of place! Oooooooh, you're so
unpredictable.

Scorpio You're emotionally intense and your feelings
run very, very deep. So deep, in fact, that it's sometimes
difficult to work you out. You have good powers of
concentration and once you get your teeth into a project
you like to see it through to the end. Learn to talk about
your feelings more, and watch out for that jealous streak!

Sagittarius For you, a spade's a spade and you can be
pretty blunt when you want to. *You* can take things on the
chin, you reason, so why can't other people? In sports,
you're championship material. In love, you're flirty and
flighty.

Capricorn You're very impressive, you know that?

You work hard, you're determined and highly ambitious. You know exactly where you're going and what you want out of life. Just remember that maxim: all work and no play makes Jack a dull boy!

Aquarius Outwardly you're friendly but you don't like to get too emotionally involved. You take great delight in shocking people. You love to watch the expression on their faces when you say something outrageous or when you turn up at a friend's house in the most outlandish outfit. You're a tease, you are!

Pisces Of all Aries personalities, you are perhaps the most sensitive and the least brash. You're shy and retiring and afraid of getting hurt. As a friend, you're wonderfully sympathetic and full of understanding. Soft and vulnerable, you're one of life's romantics.

sensible *practical*
materialistic

tower
of
strength

Taurus

solid

steady as a rock

plodding

pragmatic

obstinate **earthy**

emotionally stable and well-balanced

love of routine

creative

pleasure

money-oriented *sensual*

security-minded

slow but sure

bull in a china shop

The Bull

April 20–
May 20

shrewd **loving**

level-headed

down-to-earth

Are You A True Taurean?

Find out how typical you are of your sign. Check only **one** box for each question.

	Often	Sometimes	Never
Do you like making things?	○	◉	○
Do you get jealous?	○	○	◉
Do you spend hours in the bathroom?	○	○	◉
Do you flirt?	◉	○	○
Do people come to you for practical help or advice?	◉	○	○
Do you like going shopping?	○	◉	○
Do you like snuggling up to your boy/girlfriend, best friend, mom, etc.?	◉	○	○
Do you wish things could always stay as they are?	○	◉	○
Do you take as many opportunities as you can to sit down?	○	○	◉

	Often	Sometimes	Never
Do you boss people around?	⊙	◯	◯
How often do you eat candy, cakes or puddings?	◯	◯	⊙
Do you dream about being fabulously wealthy?	◯	⊙	◯

Score: You score 2 points for an "Often" answer, 1 point for a "Sometimes" answer, 0 points for a "Never."

0 - 12 You're not a typical Taurean, so perhaps you were born at the very beginning or at the very end of your sign, which would modify your character. If so, you're what is known as "cuspal" and are a mixture of two signs. If you were born at the very beginning of Taurus, you share some of Aries' characteristics and should read about that sign as well. If you were born at the end you share some of Gemini's characteristics, so read up on that sign too.

13 - 18 Although you do have many Taurean characteristics, your Moon placement probably modifies your character and personality quite noticeably. Find out more by reading about how the Moon affects your emotions on page 32.

19 and Over You're a true Taurean. Now read on and find out more about yourself.

Sign Associations

- **Element** – Earth
- **Lucky day** – Friday
- **Lucky number** – 6
- **Stone** – Emerald, Jade
- **Flower** – Carnation, Rose
- **Color** – Green, blue, cream
- **Taurus rules** – The neck and throat

Your Ruling Planet

As a Taurean, your ruling planet is Venus so you may be interested in some of the things associated with this planet. The symbol for Venus is:

Venus is associated with:

- *a love of art, music and drama*
- *social graces and good manners*
- *love and lovers*
- *the fashion and beauty biz.*
- *food and catering*
- *floristry*

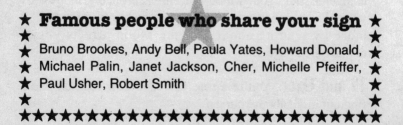

★ **Famous people who share your sign** ★

★ Bruno Brookes, Andy Bell, Paula Yates, Howard Donald, ★
★ Michael Palin, Janet Jackson, Cher, Michelle Pfeiffer, ★
★ Paul Usher, Robert Smith ★

Keynotes to Taurus

you belong to the Earth element, so: you're practical, logical and down-to-earth. You work hard. You're good with your hands. You have green thumbs.

your talents and interests lie in: art, design, music, dancing, drama, fashion, money management, craftwork, cookery, gardening.

you work: steadily and systematically at your own pace – not too fast, not too slow.

you hate: being hassled.

at school: because you don't like change very much, you take quite a long time getting used to a new class. But, give it a few weeks and you start to settle into the routine and begin to get used to the steady pace of things. And as long as you do take things steadily, everything's all right. Now and again, you might need a bit of a push – which you hate and kick furiously against – but in the long run it does help to get you up a gear. You're good at languages, history and creative arts but probably enjoy practical subjects best. You just love making things. And boy! can you talk. You could talk your way to an Olympic gold medal.

you spend your money: on candy and ice cream. Oooooh, you've got such a sweet tooth!

you like your bedroom to be: deeply luxurious. Being the little sensualist that you are, comfort is immensely important to you. You like thick shag-pile carpets, a mattress you can sink into and a nice, soft, relaxing easy chair to sit in. And the closer to the bathroom, the better. Walking down a long cold hallway in the middle of the night when you need to use the bathroom is no picnic. You like your room to look attractive, but you'll probably steer away from bold, dramatic colors. A room that is light and airy and has plenty of space to stretch out would be your ideal.

You keep fit by: er ... actually, you prefer lounging around! Strenuous exercise is not the way Taureans would choose to spend a rainy afternoon. A body massage is the closest you want to get to working your muscles. If you absolutely have to be physical, dancing or exercising to music is perhaps your best choice.

The Taurean Personality

Taureans are laid-back, affectionate and cuddly people. They're good-natured, kind, and immensely charming. And, of course, belonging to the Earth element means they're thoroughly sensible, level-headed individuals whose feet are very firmly plonked on the ground.

By a long way, the two most important things in a Taurean's life are comfort and security and there are possibly only three situations in life that will make these normally placid creatures blow their stack:
1. If they're physically uncomfortable – e.g. if their shoes pinch, or they have to sit on a hard chair, or are forced to go on a diet – that sort of thing.
2. If they're pushed – being told to speed up is like a red flag to a bull.
3. If someone threatens to take their possessions away from them – incidentally, Taureans tend to think of people

as possessions too (especially boy/girlfriends!)

Of the three, the last is perhaps the most dangerous thing to do to them, because if someone tries to put their hands on what a Taurean considers is rightfully his/hers they'll immediately turn a docile creature into a raging bull – and a raging bull is not a pretty sight!

In relationships Taureans are soft, warm and generous. They just love snuggling and cuddling. And though they can be flirty, they don't give their hearts away to just anyone, you know. Get real. They may be romantic but they're NOT silly!

If you're a Taurean, would you say this was a fair description of you?

What you really think about yourself but wouldn't dream of saying to anyone else: *I deserve an easy life.*

What you want most in the world: *To be pampered and spoiled.*

What your mom would say to you: *No wonder you were in the bathroom so long. You've been using my expensive bubble bath again, haven't you?!*

What your teacher would write in your school report: *Good, steady, reliable worker.*

What your best friend would say to you: *Here, I'll bandage your ankle for you, then you'll be out of the cross-country run this afternoon.*

How to insult a Taurean: *Get lost, you greedy pig!*

If your boyfriend is a typical Taurean...

You can spot him a mile away because he's: got a warm and friendly look about him. His face has a classically square jaw line. His eyes are often deeply set and his lips are full and red. A tell-tale sign of Taurus is curly hair which flops over a broad forehead. He may be rather chunky but this is precisely what gives him that irresistibly soft and cuddly appeal. Fashion-wise he likes to look smart, although his clothes may tend to be a little tame. Also, boys of this sign often have deeper voices than average.

- **He likes:** *food, expensive clothes, food, music, and more food!*

- **He needs:** *a steady routine.*

- **He's great because he's:** *easy-going.*

- **He's a drag because he's:** *so pig-headed.*

- **Never:** *steal anything from him.*

On your first date with him: he may come across as a bit awkward to begin with but it's only because he's a little uncomfortable with people he doesn't know. He's what you might call a slow starter so perhaps if you went out in a crowd it might help to ease some of those early jitters. Perhaps you could go to a club – he's great dancer – or take a long, slow walk in the park. Once he's more relaxed with you you'll find that he is one cuddly dude. You can be sure he'll take care of you and get you back to your house safe and sound and exactly on time – just as he promised your mom he would.

On his birthday, spoil him: with a box of expensive candy.

If your girlfriend is a typical Taurean...

You can spot her a mile away because she's: very pretty with a square-shaped, dimpled face, large eyes, soft, full lips and masses of hair. She's average in height and she loves wearing soft, flowy, comfortable clothes. Her neck is a strong feature – either because it's long and slender or because it's noticeably muscular. Because her sign rules her neck she often unconsciously draws attention to it by wearing interesting necklaces or chokers. Collars especially look great on her.

- **She likes:** *anything pretty.*

- **She needs:** *security and stability.*

- **She's great because she's:** *got such charm.*

- **She's a drag because she's:** *so stubborn.*

- **Never:** *kick away her support*

On your first date with her: you'll find out pretty quickly that this girl has got her head screwed on. She may be easy-going but she's no push-over. For a start, she'll either take to you or hate you on sight. If it's the first, she'll want to take some time to get to know you better. (If it's the latter, you can forget it, buster.) Don't screw up by moving in too quickly. Getting too physical too soon will immediately put the kiss of death on the whole thing. Take her to a movie – it must be romantic – and make sure you go past a string of shops on route. Shopping is her Numero Uno, top of the list, favorite hobby ever.

On her birthday, spoil her: by making her favorite dinner for her!

Taurus in love

❤ **You have a special understanding with:** Virgos, Capricorns and, of course, other Taureans.

❤ **In a relationship your best qualities are:** loyalty, faithfulness, ability to listen and sympathize.

❤ **In a relationship your worst qualities are:** possessiveness and jealousy.

❤ **Your ideal partner:** is someone dependable, someone you're sure you can trust and rely on completely. It's got to be a solid, sensible, down-to-earth person like yourself and if s/he is practical and good at making things, then even better. You can be a little bit of a snob when it comes to choosing who to go out with because you rather like to be seen with a popular partner at your side. And if he or she is loaded, then even better!

Dos & don'ts for happy relationships

do ✓	don't X
✓enjoy the romance of your relationship ✓build a relationship on love, not on what material goodies it will give you	X be so stodgily practical and sensible all the time X let your possessiveness stifle the life out of your partner

Your Taurus love chart

Taurus with ♥	Your relationship together ♥	At a glance
Aries	exciting but too erratic	♥♥♥
Taurus	slow and steady	♥♥♥
Gemini	stressed out	♥
Cancer	sweet and sensitive	♥♥♥♥
Leo	passionate but challenging	♥♥♥
Virgo	brilliant – go for it!	♥♥♥♥♥
Libra	classy	♥♥♥
Scorpio	attraction of opposites?	♥♥♥
Sagittarius	pretty tame	♥♥
Capricorn	simply the best!	♥♥♥♥♥
Aquarius	insecure	♥
Pisces	low-impact	♥♥♥

♥ = grim   ♥♥ = so-so   ♥♥♥ = stick with it

♥♥♥♥ = magnetic   ♥♥♥♥♥ = fwoarrrgh!

The Moon and Your Emotions

Everything you've read about yourself so far has been based on the Sun's position at the time of your birth which, in your case, was in the sign of Taurus. This tells you a great deal about your character. But if you want to know more about your emotions, you need to know in which sign the Moon was placed when you were born.

Find your Moon sign by turning to the tables on page 187 then read below how it works with your Sun sign to affect and modify your Taurean nature.

Sun in Taurus with Moon in:)) ●

Aries Though on the surface you're laid-back, this combination suggests you've got a good deal more up-and-at-'em than most other Taureans. You'll quite enjoy energetic sports and you prefer leading the crowd rather than being at the back of the line.

Taurus You're absolutely solid and steadfast, especially where friendships and loyalties are concerned. However, this may mean that you're also stubborn and pig-headed too. You have great arts, crafts and musical talents.

Gemini With this combination you have the ability to reason through your feelings and you tend to keep your head in situations where others are losing theirs. You're pretty bright and especially good at writing.

Cancer Your home and your family are likely to be the center of your universe. You probably get excellent grades and should do very well in Art and Music. You're gentler and more sensitive than most other Taureans.

Leo Put the Leonine love of gracious living together with the Taurean need for comfort and luxury and you can see how you're going to want to live life the five-star way. Singing or acting would make a great career for you.

Virgo You're highly practical, methodical and extremely efficient in your work. Because your instincts are to look after people you're a naturally caring person and you could do very well in the medical profession.

Libra You have good taste and an even greater love of creature comforts. You probably hate games and PE but you will adore painting and music. If you don't already play a musical instrument, why not start to learn one now?

Scorpio You're sensual and very sexy but you can also be selfish and intolerant too. Your aptitude for fact-finding and digging up secrets means you're terrific at any kind of investigative work. You've got what it takes to be a success.

Sagittarius You may be laid back but you can also be restless at times. So, perhaps you're more sporty than is usual for a Taurean or, if you're academic, you might be really good at study and research. You find it easy to make friends even if, at times, you can be a little tactless.

Capricorn Loyal and devoted, you're affectionate and caring of those you love. With strong practical skills you're a champion organizer. Hard-working, ambitious and shrewd, your determination to be successful may turn you into a workaholic. Admit it, you're a bit of a snob, aren't you? You like flashing status symbols and exclusive labels around.

Aquarius Your freedom to come and go and to be yourself is very important to you in life. What gives you a great deal of satisfaction is helping those less fortunate than yourself. Your intuition could make you a pioneer in creative ideas.

Pisces You're more sensitive than the average Taurean and also more imaginative. With your practical ability and staying power you could be very successful in the Arts. You could excel in music, painting, poetry, writing or craftwork.

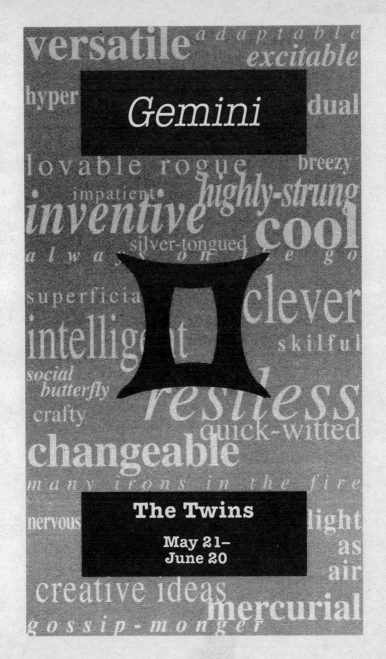

Gemini

The Twins

May 21–
June 20

versatile · adaptable · excitable · hyper · dual · lovable rogue · breezy · impatient · highly-strung · inventive · cool · silver-tongued · always on the go · superficial · clever · intelligent · skilful · social butterfly · restless · crafty · quick-witted · changeable · many irons in the fire · nervous · light as air · creative ideas · mercurial · gossip-monger

Are You A True Gemini?

Find out how typical you are of your sign. Check only **one** box for each question.

	Often	Sometimes	Never
Are you flirty and flighty?	⊙	○	○
Do you get bored easily?	⊙	○	○
Do things seem to happen to you in twos?	○	○	⊙
Do you get scolded for talking?	○	⊙	○
Do you start new hobbies and then abandon them half-way through?	⊙	○	○
Do you get nervously excited?	○	⊙	○
Do you find it difficult to switch your brain off?	⊙	○	○
Do you change your mind about things?	○	⊙	○
Do you spend hours talking to your friends on the phone?	○	⊙	○

	Often	Sometimes	Never
Do you get crazed for new things?	⊙	○	○
Do you take a lot on thinking you'll be able to do it all and then later find it's just too much to cope with?	○	⊙	○
Do you have more than one boy/girlfriend at the same time?	⊙	○	○

Score: You score 2 points for an "Often" answer, 1 point for a "Sometimes" answer, 0 points for a "Never."

0 - 12 You're not a typical Gemini, so perhaps you were born at the very beginning or at the very end of your sign, which would modify your character. If so, you're what is know as "cuspal" and are a mixture of two signs. If you were born at the very beginning of Gemini you share some Taurean characteristics and should read about that sign as well. If you were born at the end, you share some Cancerian characteristics, so read up on that sign too.

13 - 18 Although you do have many Gemini characteristics, your Moon placement probably modifies your character and personality quite noticeably. Find out more by reading about how the Moon affects your emotions on page 46.

19 and Over You're a true Gemini. Now read on and find out more about yourself.

Sign Associations

- **Element** – Air
- **Lucky day** – Wednesday
- **Lucky number** – 5
- **Stone** – Agate
- **Flower** – Honeysuckle, Lily-of-the-valley
- **Color** – White, light yellow
- **Gemini rules** – The arms and shoulders

Your Ruling Planet

As a Gemini, your ruling planet is Mercury so you may be interested in some of the things associated with this planet. The symbol for Mercury is:

Mercury is associated with:

- *communications, business and commerce*
- *journeys, travel, speed and motion*
- *computers and technical gadgets*
- *brain work, wit, humor, jokes*
- *jugglers and magicians*
- *hoaxes*

★ **Famous people who share your sign** ★

Paul Gascoigne, Kylie Minogue, Harry Enfield, Bob Monkhouse, Morrissey, Mark Goodier, Mick Hucknall, Johnny Depp, Paul McCartney, the artist formerly known as "Prince"

Keynotes to Gemini

you belong to the Air element, so: you're chatty and sociable. You're also idealistic, particularly about people. Beauty is important to you.

your talents and interests lie in: communications, computer work, broadcasting, reading, writing, acting, talking, debating, playing music, speaking foreign languages, working with anything that requires quick, skilled fingers. You're a great juggler – mentally and physically.

you work: quickly and intelligently but only for as long as you're interested in what you're doing.

you hate: the same old routine.

at school: you don't have too many problems in class because you're pretty sharp and you pick up new subjects really quickly – too quickly, because then you get bored when the teacher has to go over things for the slower ones. You're interested in lots of different subjects but you don't like to go too deeply into any of them. This means you know a little about a lot of things. But it's probably enough to get you through exams fairly easily, so tests don't pose too great a problem for you. You lose your concentration quickly, though, and spend a lot of time staring out of the window or idly chattering. Reading, writing and most of all, computer work, grab your attention the most.

you spend your money: on computer games and magazines.

you like your bedroom to be: as light and airy

as possible. It's perhaps best if your room is at the very top of the house so you can see as far as you can. You probably have your window open as often as possible, even in the heart of winter. You don't like clutter but you do have lots of half-finished kits or wacky gizmos around. Somehow, one room never seems enough for you and all your bits and pieces so you tend to spread your paraphernalia around all over the rest of the house and take over other people's rooms as well as your own.

You keep fit by: flexing the muscles of your tongue or by doing mental exercises – some of which come in handy for inventing excuses to be left out of games!

♊ ♊ ♊

The Gemini Personality

Geminis are the livewires of the Zodiac. They have the most bubbly, effervescent personality: amusing, entertaining, sparkling, witty, able to carry on four conversations at the same time, without ever losing track of what anyone is saying.

It's exhausting trying to keep up with them, though, because they flit about all over the place. Things suddenly capture their interest and they're compelled to drop whatever it is they're doing in favor of the new attraction. It has been said they have the lowest boredom threshold of all the twelve signs. That's a fancy way of saying they get bored very quickly.

Because of this, Geminians need masses of hobbies to keep their interests alive. And, for the very same reason, they need masses of friends too. There can't be a Geminian alive who doesn't have a bulging address book full of names and phone numbers. The saying, "Variety is the spice of life," must have been invented especially for them.

But just as they can be volatile and changeable about their interests, so they can be positively chameleon-like in their moods. Now and again they can be cold and distant. It all depends on how the mood grabs them. One minute they can be all over you and the next minute, well, frankly, it's all over.

Most times, though, these friendly and likeable folk are ever so easy to get on with. They have a knack of tuning in to someone's wavelength, so that everybody feels comfortable with them.

If you're Gemini-born, would you say this picture was anything like you?

What you really think about yourself but wouldn't dream of saying to anyone else: *I can outsmart anyone.*

What you want most in the world: *To write a best-seller.*

What your mom would say to you: *For Pete's sake, get off that phone, other people need to use it too, you know!*

What your teacher would write in your school report: *Easily distracted.*

What your best friend would say to you: *Go on, tell me your secret. How do you get away with so little work and still end up with top marks for your essays, eh?*

How to insult a Gemini: *You're so stupid, you dork!*

If your boyfriend is a typical Gemini...

You can spot him a mile away because he's: probably thin and gangly but by no means the tallest in the group. The thing that really gives him away is his jittery, fidgetiness – he literally can't keep still. Look for the guy who's shuffling his feet, drumming his fingers, or jingling the change in his pocket. If by some miracle he is standing still, his eyes will be doing overtime: they'll be clocking everything in sight – including that zit you thought you'd so cleverly covered with make-up this morning!

- **He likes:** *electronic gadgets.*

- **He needs:** *masses and masses of variety.*

- **He's great because he:** *can make you laugh.*

- **He's a drag because he:** *gets bored easily.*

- **Never:** *use tears to get what you want – it simply won't wash.*

On your first date with him: he'll probably flirt with you something rotten! Geminis are dreadful flirts. But don't let that put you off because he's immensely good fun and great company and you'll have a terrific time with him. He's got lots to say for himself so there won't be any of those embarrassing silences you get with some guys. He's so friendly and easygoing and with all those different interests of his, it's anybody's guess where he'll want to go on your date.

On his birthday, spoil him: by giving him the most intricate science kit you can find.

If your girlfriend is a typical Gemini...

You can spot her a mile away because she's: the most vivacious girl in the crowd – she'll be the one who's making everyone laugh! Her gestures and mannerisms are quick (bird-like, some people would say), and if she isn't waving or pointing, she's probably biting her nails. She'll be turning her head, craning her neck, so as not to miss any action. Geminis never seem to grow old so you can bet she'll look a lot younger than the rest of the crowd. And for the last giveaway clue: watch her trying to fish something out of her bag. It's so cluttered, it'll take her until tomorrow to find what she's looking for.

- **She likes:** *to do crossword puzzles.*

- **She needs:** *lots of hobbies and interests (and perhaps boyfriends) at once.*

- **She's great because she's:** *bright and cheerful.*

- **She's a drag because she's:** *so unreliable.*

- **Never:** *expect her interest in anything to last for long (and that includes you!).*

On your first date with her: be prepared to spill the beans and dish the dirt. She'll want to know everything about you and take huge delight in any gossip you can tell her. This bubbly babe will laugh and tell you amusing stories and talk about anything under the sun. She loves having fun and she needs masses of entertainment, so sit in a coffee bar and listen to her comments about the passers-by – she'll have you in stitches!

On her birthday, spoil her: by throwing a surprise party for her and inviting all her friends.

Gemini in love

♥ **You have a special understanding with:** Librans, Aquarians and, of course, other Geminis too.

♥ **In a relationship your best qualities are:** a love of fun, humor, liveliness, charm, inventiveness, attention to detail.

♥ **In a relationship your worst qualities are:** cunning, deceit, exploitation, lack of consideration.

♥ **Your ideal partner:** is someone who's on the same intellectual level as yourself, someone who can make you laugh, who can keep you guessing, who's a bit unpredictable and who'll talk with you for hours. Someone who understands that you'll want to flirt at parties but who won't make a scene because he or she knows it's not serious. When you do find a partner like that, be sure to stick to him/her like glue. Don't mess around – they don't grow on trees!

Dos & don'ts for happy relationships

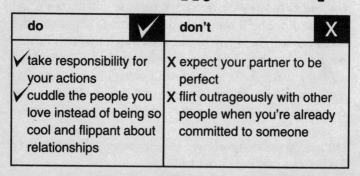

do ✓	don't ✗
✓ take responsibility for your actions ✓ cuddle the people you love instead of being so cool and flippant about relationships	✗ expect your partner to be perfect ✗ flirt outrageously with other people when you're already committed to someone

Your Gemini love chart

| Gemini with ♥ Your relationship together ♥ At a glance |

Gemini with	Your relationship together	At a glance
Aries	good fun	♥♥♥♥
Taurus	a hard job	♥
Gemini	bright and breezy	♥♥♥♥♥
Cancer	neither of you live on the same planet	♥
Leo	light and airy	♥♥
Virgo	has its promising moments	♥♥♥
Libra	gorrrrrrrgeous!	♥♥♥♥♥
Scorpio	no way, José	♥
Sagittarius	attraction of opposites?	♥♥♥
Capricorn	like going up a down-escalator	♥
Aquarius	flashy and sassy	♥♥♥♥♥
Pisces	too clingy for your liking	♥♥

♥ = grim   ♥♥ = so-so   ♥♥♥ = stick with it

♥♥♥♥ = magnetic   ♥♥♥♥♥ = fwoarrrgh!

The Moon and Your Emotions

Everything you've read about yourself so far has been based on the Sun's position at the time of your birth which, in your case, was in the sign of Gemini. This tells you a great deal about your character. But if you want to know more about your emotions, you need to know in which sign the Moon was placed when you were born.

Find your Moon sign by turning to the tables on page 187 then read below how it works with your Sun sign to affect and modify your Geminian nature.

Sun in Gemini with Moon in: ☽ ☽ ●

Aries Flighty, flirty, sexy, shirty. You've got ants in your pants and you can't keep still. You've got masses of energy and you're as curious as a cat. Brilliant at languages and communications, you'd do well in journalism or TV.

Taurus With this combination, you'll be able to settle down long enough to see through many of the projects you take on. You're very creative and come up with some pretty inventive ideas. You shine when it comes to arts and crafts.

Gemini Young at heart and youthful in body, you're the sort of person who'll never truly grow up or grow old. You're very intelligent and have brilliant ideas. Think about writing children's stories, computer games, or a career in pop music.

Cancer What a memory you've got! You can probably remember right back to year one. Of course, this should help you pass exams with little difficulty. You're much warmer, kinder and a lot more affectionate than the average Geminian.

Leo You're the belle of the ball, the talk of the town, the man of the match. Your sparkling personality will always ensure you get invited to the party. You're happiest under the spotlight, where you can perform to your heart's content.

Virgo Because you're tenacious, you're likely to get more mileage out of your inventive ideas than most of your other fellow Geminians. With your technical abilities and literary talents you should excel in writing and technical design.

Libra With this combination you should be a brilliant story-teller. You're so talkative you're in danger of becoming a gas-bag. But you're immensely charming, persuasive and diplomatic, so politics or the legal profession may attract.

Scorpio Clever and canny, you're very sharp and perceptive. You come across as street-wise with that cool-cat or slick-chick act of yours. True, you're no push-over, but then you're also much more emotional than you like to make out.

Sagittarius You have a restless mind that seeks new excitement and adventure all the time. You could find this physically, through sport, or mentally, through your schoolwork or research. You excel with foreign languages.

Capricorn With this combination, you could be good at both art and science subjects and may have difficulty deciding which to specialize in. Because you're clever, hard-working and well-organized, you'll do well in whatever you choose.

Aquarius What imagination! What creativity! What far-flung ideas! People like you make exciting inventors, at the forefront of the technological revolution. Anything to do with computers, multimedia, the internet or virtual reality should grab you.

Pisces You can be romantic and sentimental but whimsical too, so that making up your mind can sometimes be agony. With your soft, gentle, and tender heart, you could write dreamy love stories or become a leading fashion designer.

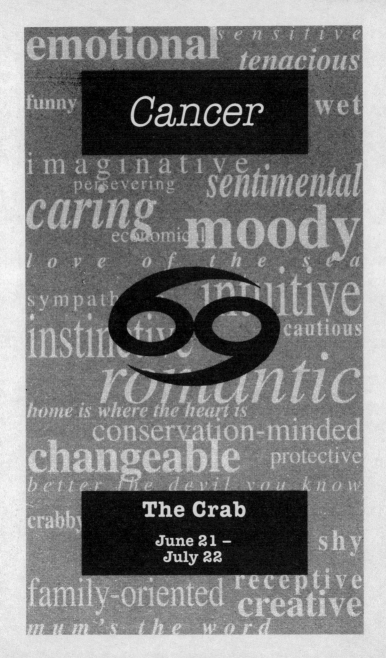

emotional sensitive tenacious

funny

Cancer

wet

imaginative
persevering sentimental

caring economical moody

love of the sea

sympath intuitive

instinctive cautious

romantic

home is where the heart is

conservation-minded

changeable protective

better the devil you know

crabby

The Crab

June 21 –
July 22

shy

family-oriented receptive creative

mum's the word

Are You A True Cancerian?

Find out how typical you are of your sign. Check only **one** box for each question.

	Often	Sometimes	Never
Do you do things just to please other people?	○	○	○
Do you get upset easily?	○	○	○
Do you take what people say to you very personally?	○	○	○
Are you shy?	○	○	○
Do you like to read or watch romance stories?	○	○	○
Do you cook?	○	○	○
Do you buy romantic, sentimental or old-fashioned things?	○	○	○
Do people accuse you of being moody?	○	○	○
Do you cuddle up to your mom, dad, pussycat, teddy, boy/girlfriend?	○	○	○

	Often	Sometimes	Never
Do you tend to tidy up?	○	○	○
If someone is hurt or upset, do you want to run and help them?	○	○	○
Does the thought of being alone upset you?	○	○	○

Score: You score 2 points for an "Often" answer, 1 point for a "Sometimes" answer, 0 points for a "Never."

0 - 12 You're not a typical Cancerian so perhaps you were born at the very beginning or at the very end of your sign, which would modify your character. If so, you're what is known as "cuspal" and are a mixture of two signs. If you were born at the very beginning of Cancer, you share some of Gemini's characteristics and should read about that sign as well. If you were born at the end, you share some of Leo's characteristics, so read up on that sign too.

13 - 18 Although you do have many Cancerian characteristics, your Moon placement probably modifies your character and personality quite noticeably. Find out more by reading about how the Moon affects your emotions on page 60.

19 and Over You're a true Cancerian. Now read on and find out more about yourself.

Sign Associations

- **Element** – Water
- **Lucky day** – Monday
- **Lucky number** – 2
- **Stone** – Moonstone
- **Flower** – Lily
- **Color** – Silver, green
- **Cancer rules** – The chest, breast and stomach

Your Ruling Planet

As a Cancerian, your ruling planet is the Moon and so you may be interested in some of the things associated with this planet. The symbol for the Moon is:

The Moon is associated with:

- *moods, emotions and impressions*
- *females and, especially, the mother*
- *the general public*
- *intuition, memory and imagination*
- *a need for change*
- *fluids, water and the tides*

★ **Famous people who share your sign** ★

Princess Diana, Tom Hanks, Bill Cosby, George Michael, Jerry Hall, Tom Cruise, Sylvester Stallone, Pauline Quirke, Jason Orange, Robin Williams, Chris O'Donnell, Bill Oddie

Keynotes to Cancer

you belong to the **Water** *element, so:* you're sensitive, emotionally intense and your heart often rules your head. You enjoy messing around in or near water.

your **talents** *and* **interests** *lie in:* cooking and catering, gardening, children, water sports, interior decorating and design, furniture making, collecting things.

you **work:** intuitively. Cancerians have excellent memories which come in nice and handy at exam time, thank you very much.

you **hate:** being mocked.

at **school:** let's face it, you'd simply rather stay at home, wouldn't you? As far as you're concerned the best thing about school is the holidays. Remember when you cried every single morning of that first year of kindergarten? Even now you'll find any excuse to take the odd day off. Food, at least, is comforting and the promise of lunchtime just about keeps you going through the morning. Home schooling would suit you. Boarding school would break your heart.

you spend your **money:** carefully. Actually, you're very canny with money and prefer to put it in your piggy bank than spend it on things you don't need.

you like your **bedroom** *to be:* light and shiny. You're happier in a room that's painted white with perhaps touches of blue or green. Two things will stand out. First, there's your love of the sea, so you may have shell-covered boxes or objects that remind you of the seaside.

And second, you're sentimental so you may have lots of memorabilia around. Perhaps things that used to belong to your mom or your grandad when they were young – an old teddy or a picture that would have hung in their bedroom when they were your age.

you keep *fit* by: swimming, canoeing, surfing – anything, in fact, that gets you wet.

The Cancerian Personality

Cancerians love cocooning themselves in their homes. They're very attached to their family and home environment. This is where they feel safest and most comfortable. Like sand crabs, they dig themselves in and the thought of uprooting themselves again and leaving behind all the things that are so familiar to them, is very unsettling indeed.

They make excellent cooks – just as well since they love food! They have green thumbs and enjoy puttering around the house. One of their favorite pastimes is collecting things, particularly objects of sentimental value. Actually, it's not really collecting. It's more like hoarding. If it came to a contest between them and the squirrels, don't put your money on our bushy-tailed friends.

Cancer-born folk have amazing memories – they never forget anything. And what they love to remember most is their early childhood. They never get tired of hearing stories about themselves when they were little. Emotionally, Cancerians are very tender and they get hurt easily. Things that perhaps someone else wouldn't think twice about, can upset them deeply. That's probably because they're a tad prone to reading more into a situation than is necessary, and then leaping to quite the wrong conclusions. When that happens, they retreat smartly behind their protective shells. And this is what gives them their reputation for being moody or crabby.

Whether male or female, old or young, Cancerians are naturally caring, protective and loyal. But by far and away, the most important influence in their own lives has to be – their moms.

If you're one of these tender Crabs, would you agree?

What you really think about yourself but wouldn't dream of saying to anyone else: *I'm afraid of the whole wide world.*

What you want most in the world: *An old manor house all of your own.*

What your mom would say to you: *Why don't you go over to a friend's house instead of getting under my skin all day long?*

What your teacher would write in your school report: *Tidy and well-organized.*

What your best friend would say to you: *Hey, you're good at remembering things. What was that formula we're supposed to learn by heart for Chemistry?*

How to insult a Cancerian: *Why don't you run home to mommy, you boring dweeb?*

If your boyfriend is a typical Cancerian...

You can spot him a mile away because he's: got a distinctive round face and paler skin than average (don't forget, he's ruled by the Moon!). He's of average height, fairly hunky and he wears lots of soft, comfy clothes like woolly sweaters which make him look all soft and squashy – a bit like your favorite cuddly teddy bear.

- **He likes:** *his mom.*

- **He needs:** *TLC (tender loving care).*

- **He's great because he's:** *easy to talk to.*

- **He's a drag because he's:** *so sappy.*

- **Never:** *criticize him cruelly.*

On your first date with him: he'll probably want to take you home to meet the family. Since the way to this guy's heart is definitely through his stomach, why not suggest going out for a pizza instead? He may look big and butch but he's a real softy and ever so sentimental. He goes all gooey if he sees little fluffy ducklings in the river, or furry baby animals at the zoo, or even if anyone mentions that word – love. Aaaah! Isn't he irresistible?

On his birthday, spoil him: by giving him a toy puppy that he can cuddle.

If your girlfriend is a typical Cancerian...

You can spot her a mile away because she's: so pretty and feminine. She has a sweet little nose that turns up at the tip. Although she's shy and not very tall, she stands out because she's so cute and soft-looking. She wears very feminine clothes, in her favorite blue-green colors.

- **She likes:** *silvery things.*

- **She needs:** *someone strong to lean on.*

- **She's great because she's:** *so understanding.*

- **She's a drag because she's:** *always putting herself down.*

- **Never:** *tease her maliciously.*

On your first date with her: she's a sensitive flower so she'll require delicate handling. She needs respect and certainly won't appreciate bad manners or any rough stuff, you know. She likes her guys to be manly but refined and to know how to treat her like a lady. She may be a shy violet, but this gal's all female. Take her to a romantic movie or sit in the park and share a big bag of chips between you and just talk and talk . . .

On her birthday, spoil her: by taking her to the seaside for the day.

Cancer in love

♥ **You have a special understanding with:** Scorpios, Pisces and, of course, other Cancerians.

♥ **In a relationship your best qualities are:** sensitivity and protectiveness towards those you love.

♥ **In a relationship your worst qualities are:** grumpiness, over-dependency and an unforgiving nature.

♥ **Your ideal partner:** is someone who likes life to revolve around the home, who enjoys trips to the seaside and, above all, who won't mind if your mother tags along, too.

Dos & don'ts for happy relationships

do ✔	don't ✗
✔ learn to be more independent	✗ keep saying you prefer your mom's cooking!
✔ sort out any problems before they get out of hand	✗ stay in all the time – find some interests that take you out of the house more

Your Cancer love chart

Cancer with ♥	Your relationship together ♥	At a glance
Aries	not many highlights	♥
Taurus	groovy	♥♥♥♥
Gemini	forget it!	♥
Cancer	cozy twosome	♥♥♥♥
Leo	steamy	♥♥♥
Virgo	yeah! lots going for it	♥♥♥♥
Libra	all downhill	♥♥
Scorpio	phew!	♥♥♥♥♥
Sagittarius	just possible	♥♥
Capricorn	attraction of opposites?	♥♥♥
Aquarius	icy-cold	♥
Pisces	seventh heaven	♥♥♥♥♥

♥ = grim   ♥♥ = so-so   ♥♥♥ = stick with it

♥♥♥♥ = magnetic   ♥♥♥♥♥ = fwoarrrgh!

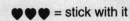

The Moon and Your Emotions

Everything you've read about yourself so far has been based on the Sun's position at the time of your birth which, in your case, was in the sign of Cancer. This tells you a great deal about your character. But if you want to know more about your emotions, you need to know in which sign the Moon was placed when you were born.

Find your Moon sign by turning to the tables on page 187 then read below how it works with your Sun sign to affect and modify your Cancerian nature.

Sun in Cancer with Moon in:

Aries The Moon in Aries means you're not quite as sappy and sensitive as your fellow Cancerians might be. But you're restless and more competitive too, so you could be very good at sports.

Taurus A soft, comfortable home becomes even more important for you with the Moon placed here. You're great at art and you adore music. Perhaps you can sing, or dance or play an instrument. You're an ace at practical subjects.

Gemini You are able to handle your emotions a good deal more rationally with this Moon placement, which should make life a lot easier. Your restlessness means that changes won't be so upsetting. You're intuitively clever.

Cancer With this combination, you could be ultra tender, sensitive and emotional. Family life is doubly important to you, so is the protection of being surrounded by loved ones. You're brilliant at caring for and looking after others.

Leo Although emotionally sensitive, you do like being in the limelight. You're likely to be charming, loving and lovable and you go out of your way to please others. Luxury is important and a career on the stage is tempting.

Virgo A brilliant combination which would help you tremendously in any practical work or if you wanted to go into the medical profession. The Virgo Moon suggests you tend to worry too much, though, especially over silly details.

Libra A very suave combination, this, giving you plenty of charm and elegance. Perhaps you play a musical instrument or maybe you have a good singing voice. If so, join the school orchestra or choir.

Scorpio You can appear ever so tough and determined on the surface and few would realize the depths that your emotions can go to. With this combination you're very, very sensitive, so your shell has to be ultra thick!

Sagittarius A Sagittarian Moon here means that you're able to lighten up more easily than most of your fellow Cancerians. With this combination you want to be on the move, explore and have adventures. Life should be more fun. In a relationship, you'll want a partner who's very loving but who'll also give you space.

Capricorn Shrewd, patient and intuitive, you have quite an old head on young shoulders. Because you're brilliant at handling responsibility and taking charge, you often find yourself put into positions of leadership and authority. You may come across as tough but in reality, you're all heart.

Aquarius You have a clever mind and can come up with some astoundingly inventive ideas. At times you're not sure whether it's your head that should rule your heart or the other way around. Find your balance.

Pisces Both your Sun and Moon are in Water signs, which makes you super-sensitive. So you have stunning intuition, and can almost tap into other people's thoughts and feelings like a mind-reader. Capitalize on your imagination and tendency to day-dream by turning your thoughts and feelings into poems or short stories.

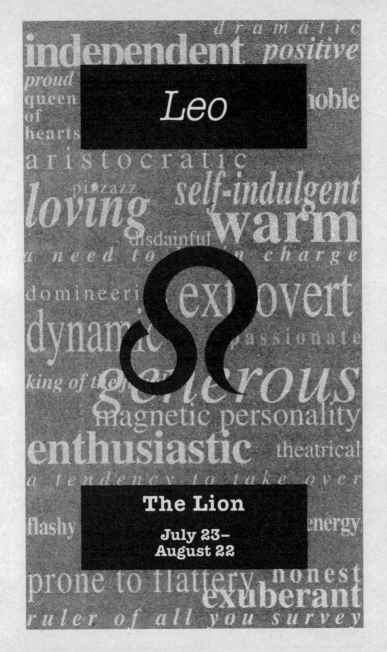

dramatic
positive
independent
proud
queen of hearts
noble
aristocratic
pizzazz
loving
self-indulgent
warm
disdainful
a need to be in charge
domineering
extrovert
dynamic
passionate
king of the jungle
generous
magnetic personality
enthusiastic
theatrical
a tendency to take over
flashy
energy

Leo

The Lion

July 23–
August 22

prone to flattery
honest
exuberant
ruler of all you survey

Are You A True Leo?

Find out how typical you are of your sign. Check only **one** box for each question.

	Often	Sometimes	Never
When you go shopping, do you buy things you like, regardless of how much they cost?	○	○	○
Are you honest?	○	○	○
Are you afraid of failure?	○	○	○
Are you proud of the things you make?	○	○	○
When you meet people do you think they find you attractive?	○	○	○
Do you get excited?	○	○	○
Do you get upset if you're ignored?	○	○	○
Do you prefer to be in the company of others rather than being on your own?	○	○	○
Do you hate people making fun of you?	○	○	○

	Often	Sometimes	Never
Do you need to be taken seriously?	○	○	○
Do you expect your friends to give you loyalty, respect and support?	○	○	○
Do you think of yourself as romantic (if you're female) or as a swash-buckling hero (if you're male)?	○	○	○

Score: You score 2 points for an "Often" answer, 1 point for a "Sometimes" answer, 0 points for a "Never."

0 - 12 You're not a typical Leo so perhaps you were born at the very beginning or at the very end of your sign which would modify your character. If so, you're what is know as "cuspal" and are a mixture of two signs. If you were born at the very beginning of Leo, you share some Cancerian characteristics and should read up on that sign. If you were born at the end, you share some of Virgo's characteristics, so read up on that sign.

13 - 18 Although you do have many Leo characteristics, your Moon placement probably modifies your character and personality quite noticeably. Find out more by reading about how the Moon affects your emotions on page 74.

19 and Over You're a true Leo. Now read on and find out more about yourself.

Sign Associations

- **Element** – Fire
- **Lucky day** – Sunday
- **Lucky number** – 1
- **Stone** – Ruby
- **Flower** – Poppy
- **Color** – Gold, flame orange, bright yellow
- **Leo rules** – The heart and back

Your Ruling Planet

As a Leo, your ruling planet is the Sun (though really it's a star) so you may be interested in some of the things associated with this planet. The symbol for the Sun is:

The Sun is associated with:

- *the ego*
- *fire, heat, warmth and passion*
- *energy, vitality and health*
- *kings, queens, royalty and nobility*
- *cats – from regal lions to common housecats*
- *celebrities and famous people*
- *gold*

★ **Famous people who share your sign** ★

The Queen of England, Arnold Schwarzenegger, Madonna, Terry Wogan, Brian Harvey, Whitney Houston, Steve Martin, Christian Slater, Patrick Swayze, Sean Penn, Ian McGaskill, Dean Cain, Sandra Bullock

Keynotes to Leo

you belong to the *Fire* element, so: you're enthusiastic, warm, open, generous and friendly. You're noisy and extroverted.

your *talents* and *interests* lie in: the dramatic arts, entertaining, dance, design, fashions, giving people hope and inspiration, the beauty biz.

you *work*: much better with a bit of praise.

you *hate*: being ridiculed.

at *school*: as long as you're popular and have a good crowd of friends, you'll like going to school. With your competitive nature you'll enjoy sports and play to win. You'll also compete in class for good marks because you don't like to be outshone. Sometimes you can be pretty lazy and just coast along but as soon as you see others getting way in front, you'll put on a dramatic spurt and get to the top again. In school, as in all things, you prefer to be asked to do something rather than told to do it.

you spend your *money*: lavishly. You never skimp when buying presents for those you love. Whoever it is you're buying for, you always try to get the best you can afford. (Leo men grow up to be sugar daddies!) When you're not spending money on other people, you buy sweets for yourself.

you like your *bedroom* to be: plush. Really, you'd like to live in a palace. The more warmth and sunshine you can get into your room, the better. You'll use golds, oranges and warm yellows to make your lair sizzle.

You keep fit by: excelling at sports.

$\Omega \quad \Omega \quad \Omega$

The Leo Personality

If you've ever lived with a cat, you'll know a thing or two about the feline mentality. How cute and cuddly little kittens can be, how playful and affectionate. You'll know, too, they can also be independent, demanding, haughty, majestic creatures. They grumble and turn their noses up if they don't like what's going on and become fierce monsters if any other cat should dare to invade their space.

On the other hand, they're graceful and slinky and always seem to land on their feet. Just give them a bit of love and attention and stroke them on the head, and you're guaranteed they'll purr with pleasure and nestle themselves in your lap for hours.

And this pretty well sums up the Leo personality. Just like cats, all Leos like to dominate the scene. They're born leaders and simply have to take charge of whatever is going on. They're show-offs because, more than anything, they like to be noticed, to be at the center of things, to be made a fuss of. When they are, they're warm and lovely and sunshiny and terrific fun to be with. But, if they're ignored, they can be sulky and disgruntled just like an old lion with a thorn in his paw.

If you're one of these pussy-cats, notice any resemblance? Come on, own up!

What you really think about yourself but wouldn't dream of saying to anyone else: *I'm terrific.*

What you want most in the world: *To be a famous actor or super mega-star.*

What your mom would say to you: *You don't think the choker is overkill, dear? After all, you are already wearing long, dangly earrings and four necklaces.*

What your teacher would write in your school report: *A born leader.*

What your best friend would say to you: *Loan me a few bucks, will you? I've forgotten my lunch money again.*

How to insult a Leo: *Get lost, you loud-mouthed poser!*

If your boyfriend is a typical Leo...

You can spot him a mile away because he's: tall, strong, physically fit and looks like one of those surfers you see in the Australian soaps. Because he's such a popular guy, he's hardly ever alone so he'll be surrounded by a crowd of guys and he'll be the one who's standing right in the middle, with his head held high. His face reminds you of a lion, with prominent cheekbones tapering down to a narrow, sometimes slightly receding, chin. There are no two ways about it – Leos have expensive tastes and you can tell that by the sort of clothes they wear. If you still haven't picked him out there's one sure telltale sign left – Leos have narrow hips and the cutest little butts you're ever likely to see!

- **He likes:** *the best.*

- **He needs:** *you to make him feel ten feet tall.*

- **He's great because he's:** *terrifically affectionate.*

- **He's a drag because he's:** *a dreadful show-off.*

- **Never:** *put him down.*

On your first date with him: he'll sweep you off your feet! This guy is a true knight in shining armor – he's courteous, protective, generous and warm-hearted. He knows how to show a girl a good time. But he'll expect you to put on a show and wear your very best outfit. He'll want to be proud of you and he'll want to see heads turning as you walk by. That way, he can bask in the glory of everyone's admiring glances.

On his birthday, spoil him: by giving him the best dinner you can. Since you probably won't be able to take him out to the Ritz (which he would enjoy very much indeed), why not bribe your mom or dad to cook something special for you, and then bribe them both to go out for the evening. Send him a formal, gilt-edged invitation card, tell him he must dress up, or else. Don't forget the candles, the best glasses and as much silver cutlery as you can put on the table before it collapses under the weight.

If your girlfriend is a typical Leo...

You can spot her a mile away because she's: the one with lots of flowing hair which she tosses like a mane. Her face looks like a cat's, with almond-shaped eyes that slant upwards at the temples. Her cheekbones are distinctive and high up and her lips, especially the bottom one, will be full. Leo's image is very important and she'll wear flamboyant clothes, in strong colors, that make a bold theatrical statement. She likes make-up and clanking jewelry – to remind you she's around just in case by chance you hadn't noticed.

- **She likes:** *compliments.*

- **She needs:** *to be told she's brilliant.*

- **She's great because she's:** *warm and generous.*

- **She's a drag because she's:** *a right old bossy boots!*

- **Never:** *laugh at her – with her, yes. At her, never!*

On your first date with her: do remember that your feline lass loves gallantry, so turn up with a single red rose wrapped in cellophane just for her. She likes glitter and glamor too, so you could take her to the swankiest club you know, but when you're dealing with Leo gals, it's not so much what you do but how you do it. You must make her feel special. Tell her she looks terrific and that you're really psyched she's going out with you. Lavish her with compliments, recite a love poem, sing her a song and drop her name into the lyrics. She has expensive tastes but at the same time, she loves having fun. So pull out all the stops and spare no expense to make this a date that will be fixed in her memory banks forever.

On her birthday, spoil her: by arranging a party for her.

Leos in love

♥ **You have a special understanding with:**
Aries, Sagittarians and, of course, other Leos.

♥ **In a relationship your best qualities are:**
passion, enthusiasm, playfulness, a spontaneous sense of
fun.

♥ **In a relationship your worst qualities are:**
hogging the limelight, haughtiness, laziness.

♥ **Your ideal partner:** is someone with drop-dead
good looks, who turns heads everwhere you go. Someone
you can see others would give their eye teeth for. At the
same time, to be an ideal partner, this person must be
someone who loves and adores you (whatever your faults
may be), who puts you on a pedestal and who would never,
whatever the circumstances, try to outshine you. A pretty
tall order, huh?

Dos & don'ts for happy relationships

do ✔	don't ✗
✔ learn to compromise	✗ let your pride get in the way
✔ give your partner a share of the limelight	✗ let possessiveness drive a good relationship away

Your Leo love chart

♌

Leo with ♥	Your relationship together ♥	At a glance
Aries	like two live wires!	♥♥♥♥♥
Taurus	strong and sexy	♥♥♥
Gemini	light-hearted	♥♥
Cancer	steamy	♥♥♥
Leo	passionate	♥♥♥♥♥
Virgo	on the edge	♥
Libra	too many differences	♥
Scorpio	powerful	♥♥♥♥
Sagittarius	sassy!	♥♥♥♥♥
Capricorn	gritty but glossy	♥♥♥
Aquarius	attraction of opposites?	♥♥♥
Pisces	it could figure	♥♥♥

♥ = grim   ♥♥ = so-so   ♥♥♥ = stick with it

♥♥♥♥ = magnetic   ♥♥♥♥♥ = fwoarrrgh!

The Moon and Your Emotions

Everything you've read about yourself so far has been based on the Sun's position at the time of your birth which, in your case, was in the sign of Leo. This tells you a great deal about your character. But if you want to know more about your emotions, you need to know in which sign the Moon was placed when you were born.

Find your Moon sign by turning to the tables on page 187 then read below how it works with your Sun sign to affect and modify your Leo nature.

Sun in Leo with Moon in:))●

Aries Phew! You're probably the most energetic person in the universe. Fiery, pacy, bold and brave. Slowing down for just a minute might give you the chance to see things from someone else's point of view. Learn how nice it can be to give in life as well as to take – that's what makes relationships happy and successful.

Taurus Common sense and a practical turn of mind go with this combination. You're probably ambitious and prepared to work hard to afford the luxury and the very best things in life that your character needs.

Gemini You're likely to be clever and alert with a mind that buzzes all over the place. You need a lot of different hobbies because you're interested in so many different things. You're great at parties because you're never lost for something to say.

Cancer Hugely loving and affectionate, your home and your family are pretty important to you. You're caring and thoughtful towards those you love and you're terrifically kind to children and animals. Emotionally, you bruise easily.

Leo You're an extrovert through and through. Take drama at school, if you can, or join the local amateur dramatics society – you'll love it! That way, you can show off to your heart's content and, what's more, you'll get applauded for it too.

Virgo You're likely to work hard and stick at a task more than most other Leos you know. As with all earthy Moon combinations, you'll have a strong streak of practicality and common-sense. A tad picky at times, though.

Libra You're image is terrifically important to you so you'll spend a lot of time getting your style just right. The grungy, seamy side of life can get you down because beauty and balance and harmony is what you aim for.

Scorpio Sunny and outward-going on the surface; deep, sensitive and passionate underneath. You can be moody and brood for ages over the smallest slight. But you're fearsomely loyal and protective of those you love.

Sagittarius Enthusiasm and a love of excitement and adventure are the keywords to this combination. You're restless and simply hate being crowded. For you, freedom is where it's at. You'll excel at sports and games.

Capricorn You're ambitious and prepared to work hard to get where you want. Perhaps you dream of being famous – a superstar actor, a model or a newsreader who's on TV every night. With this combination, you could well make it one day.

Aquarius You're taste in clothes is unconventional and pretty far-out. If you think something is unfair, you'll become passionate about it and do all you can to change things. You could become a very successful campaigner one day.

Pisces With your sensitivity you're likely to be more thoughtful and less selfish than other Leos. Perhaps you do have your head a bit in the clouds but, with your talents, you can bring those fantasies alive. Try acting or writing.

Virgo

The Maiden

August 23–
September 22

Are You A True Virgo?

Find out how typical you are of your sign. Check only **one** box for each question.

	Often	Sometimes	Never
Are you selective about your diet?	◯	◯	◯
Do you prefer to work quietly and on your own?	◯	◯	◯
Do you like doing work that requires precision and attention to fine detail?	◯	◯	◯
Are you fussy about your appearance?	◯	◯	◯
Do you worry about your health?	◯	◯	◯
Do you get bored easily?	◯	◯	◯
When you're anxious about something, do you get a stomach ache?	◯	◯	◯
Do you prefer fashion that's understated rather than loud and brash?	◯	◯	◯
Do you find parting from your friends very difficult?	◯	◯	◯

	Often	Sometimes	Never
Does it irritate you when things aren't, or don't go, right?	○	○	○
Do you lack self-confidence?	○	○	○
Do you think of yourself as a canny chick (if you're female) or a shrewd dude (if you're male)?	○	○	○

Score: You score 2 points for an "Often" answer, 1 point for a "Sometimes" answer, 0 points for a "Never."

0 - 12 You're not a typical Virgo, so perhaps you were born at the very beginning or at the very end of your sign, which would modify your character. If so, you're what is known as "cuspal" and are a mixture of two signs. If you were born at the very beginning of Virgo, you share some of Leo's characteristics and should read up that sign. If you were born at the end, you share some Libran characteristics, so have a look at that sign too.

13 - 18 Although you do have many Virgo characteristics, your Moon placement probably modifies your character and personality quite noticeably. Find out more by reading about how the Moon affects your emotions on page 88.

19 and Over You're a true Virgo. Now read on and find out more about yourself.

Sign Associations

- **Element** – Earth
- **Lucky day** – Wednesday
- **Lucky number** – 5
- **Stone** – Sardonyx
- **Flower** – Anemone
- **Color** – Dark green, blue or brown
- **Virgo rules** – The bowels and the belly

Your Ruling Planet

As a Virgo, your ruling planet is Mercury so you may be interested in some of the things that are associated with this planet. The symbol for Mercury is:

Mercury is associated with:

- *communications, languages, business and commerce*
- *journeys, travel, speed and motion*
- *computers and technical gadgets*
- *wit, humor, jokes*
- *jugglers and magicians*
- *hoaxes*

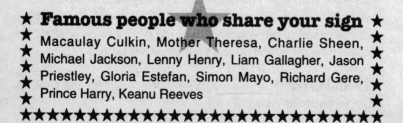

★ **Famous people who share your sign** ★

Macaulay Culkin, Mother Theresa, Charlie Sheen, Michael Jackson, Lenny Henry, Liam Gallagher, Jason Priestley, Gloria Estefan, Simon Mayo, Richard Gere, Prince Harry, Keanu Reeves

Keynotes to Virgo

you belong to the Earth element, so: you're practical, logical and down-to-earth. You work hard. You're good with your hands. You have green thumbs.

your talents and interests lie in: teaching, money management, journalism, cooking, health and diet, massage and healing, working with textiles.

you work: with an eye for detail and perfection.

you hate: anything showy or ostentatious.

at school: you're a bit of a snot. You're the person who gets his/her work put up on the wall, or who always gets merit marks for neat handwriting. You're a hard worker and a good all-rounder. You can turn your hand to almost any practical subject and get high marks for it. But then you're also clever and studious and, because you like learning, you tend to enjoy the academic side of school life as well. Conservation is a favourite topic of yours; learning about the world's natural resources, campaigning for endangered species, and animal rights are all subjects close to your heart.

you spend your money: carefully and wisely. You often make out as if you don't have a lot to spend, while in fact, your pocket money is mounting up nicely in your piggybank. When you do shell it out, you try to keep conservation or the earth's resources in mind, so you like to buy "green" or healthy products whenever you can.

you like your bedroom to be: facing the garden or overlooking some trees or green fields. If that's not possible, you like to bring the countryside indoors by having a plant or some dried flowers on a shelf. You like earthy tones in your room, like brown or splashes of green, or you may feel more restful with deep blues. You might even want to get rid of your carpet and sand your floorboards so that the bare wood will keep you in touch with nature.

you keep fit by: going for long walks, bike rides or cross-country running. At school you may find you're particularly good at gym or athletics.

♍ ♍ ♍

The Virgo Personality

Of all the signs of the Zodiac, Virgos are the most un-assuming people in the universe. As a rule, they aren't brash, or extroverted. They don't show off, have extravagant tastes or strut around like peacocks. They're not raucous and don't feel a need to draw attention to themselves.

Yet, underneath this understated personality lies a clever, capable and hard-working individual with high standards of excellence and a genius for seeing through people and for reading between the lines. If you know a Virgo, don't even try lying to him or her, and don't bother putting on any airs and graces in front of them either. They'll have chewed you out long before you've gotten close enough to see the whites of their eyes. And because they're so witty, it isn't half fun watching them cut pompous people down to size – it's not for nothing that Virgos are known as the Masters and Mistresses of the scathing put-down!

Being ruled by Mercury means that Virgos have a razor-sharp brain and they pick things up in an instant. With their refined eye for detail and acute sense of discrimination, they notice mistakes and flaws that other people wouldn't spot in a month of Sundays. Problem is, they find it hard not to point out those faults and this has earned them a reputation for being hypercritical and sharp-tongued.

Intelligent, insightful and champion organizers, Virgos have a flair for getting to the core of a problem or for finding a logical solution to a predicament. Anyone who needs advice or who ever finds him or herself in a jam, whether physical or emotional, couldn't do better than get a Virgo to sort it all out for them.

If you're a Virgo, does the cap fit?

What you really think about yourself but wouldn't dream of saying to anyone else: *I wish I were perfect.*

What you want most in the world: *To become a brain surgeon.*

What your mom would say to you: *Will you stop picking over your food and just eat your dinner like everyone else!*

What your teacher would write in your school report: *Diligent.*

What your best friend would say to you: *Lend me your notes at recess, will you? I didn't do my homework last night and the teacher said if I don't hand it in by lunchtime, he'll give me double detention.*

How to insult a Virgo: *Bug off, you tragic drama queen.*

If your boyfriend is a typical Virgo...

You can spot him a mile away because he's: tallish, stick-thin – actually, he tends to be fairly bony. He has a high forehead and bright eyes. Although he's reserved, and could never show off to save his life, you can see he doesn't miss a thing. Those shiny eyes of his are clocking everything that's going on. If you're looking for him in a crowd, look for the quiet guy who's standing at the edge of the group, the one who's neatly dressed. Does he have a spanking clean shirt on without a single crease in sight? He has? Well, that's your man!

- **He likes:** *witty jokes.*

- **He needs:** *to loosen up.*

- **He's great because he:** *is able to draw out your problems and then gives you constructive advice about how to deal with them.*

- **He's a drag because he:** *constantly interrupts you to correct what you're saying.*

- **Never:** *make him promises you can't keep.*

On your first date with him: this dude's very picky about whom he dates so, if he's asked you out, you're half-way to your first stripe already. He's no air-head, so he'll like the fact that you're interesting to talk to, that you're witty and can make him laugh. Don't come on too strong, though, he doesn't appreciate pushiness. If, after the first date, he asks you out again, you can be sure you've made the grade!

On his birthday, spoil him: by giving him the best diary or personal organizer you can afford.

If your girlfriend is a typical Virgo...

You can spot her a mile away because she's: got a pretty oval-shaped face with a little pointed nose. If she's in a crowd, she won't be the liveliest, or the noisiest and her clothes certainly won't be the brightest. But you can pick her out because she'll be the most demure. She doesn't like to draw attention to herself and prefers to wear more subdued colors. But her clothes will always be clean and unrumpled – even after a whole day at school! She doesn't wear a lot of make-up or extravagant jewelry and she somehow always succeeds in appearing graceful and dignified.

- **She likes:** *intelligent conversation.*

- **She needs:** *to feel appreciated.*

- **She's great because she's:** *tactful.*

- **She's a drag because she's:** *awfully picky.*

- **Never:** *make lewd remarks to her.*

On your first date with her: because first impressions are so important to a Virgo, you must put on a good show on your first time out together. If you don't do things right, it's unlikely you'll get a second chance because this maiden won't hesitate to ditch you. She may be a bit stand-offish to begin with but give her time and she'll mellow out beautifully. Go for a long walk or a bike ride, or visit a museum or an art gallery – this is one smart cookie so you can be sure she won't be lost for words.

On her birthday, spoil her: with a basket filled with gorgeously scented potpourri, fragrant soaps and some deliciously perfumed bubble bath.

Virgos in love

♥ **You have a special understanding with:**
Taureans, Capricorns and, of course, other Virgos.

♥ **In a relationship your best qualities are:**
remembering little details, such as your partner's favorite color, collar size or phone number.

♥ **In a relationship your worst qualities are:**
nit-picking, a cynical tongue, a tendency to nag and a reluctance to tell your partner you love him/her.

♥ **Your ideal partner:** is someone who's brainy but also practical. Someone who's emotionally solid, stable and laid back. Who'll make you feel relaxed enough to let your hair down and give you space to let off steam now and again.

Dos & don'ts for happy relationships

do ✔	don't ✗
✔ accept people, warts 'n' all	✗ be so hypercritical
✔ chill out more often	✗ be afraid to show you're tender

Your Virgo love chart

Virgo with	♥ Your relationship together ♥	At a glance
Aries	a bumpy ride	♥♥
Taurus	solid!	♥♥♥♥♥
Gemini	hit 'n' miss	♥♥♥
Cancer	can be great	♥♥♥♥
Leo	a total turn off	♥
Virgo	loads in common	♥♥♥♥♥
Libra	think again	♥
Scorpio	frustrating	♥♥
Sagittarius	on different planets	♥
Capricorn	the jackpot!	♥♥♥♥♥
Aquarius	unpredictable	♥♥
Pisces	attraction of opposites?	♥♥♥

♥ = grim ♥♥ = so-so ♥♥♥ = stick with it

♥♥♥♥ = magnetic ♥♥♥♥♥ = fwoarrrgh!

The Moon and Your Emotions

Everything you've read about yourself so far has been based on the Sun's position at the time of your birth which, in your case, was in the sign of Virgo. This tells you a great deal about your character. But if you want to know more about your emotions, you need to know in which sign the Moon was placed when you were born.

Find your Moon sign by turning to the tables on page 187 then read below how it works with your Sun sign to affect and modify your Virgoan nature.

Sun in Virgo with Moon in:

Aries You're bright and sharp and you throw yourself into your work with great gusto but you can get bored quickly and leave projects hanging in midair while you chase something more exciting. Get your ideas down on paper.

Taurus You are charming, affectionate and kind. This combination helps you to become more rational and sensible. Level-headed and with plenty of common sense, you're interested in anything connected with diet and health. Your Taurean Moon makes you immensely stubborn and once you've decided to dig in your heels, it's pointless trying to get you to change your mind.

Gemini With the Moon in Gemini, you could well be a silver-tongued devil! You're immensely clever and witty and never for a moment lost for words. You could become a good writer but take care not to upset people by what you say.

Cancer Warm and caring with a deep love for your family and home. Friends and familiar places are very important to you because you get so attached to them. You're a bit of a worrier and need to learn to unwind.

Leo You tend to like the limelight more than most other Virgos, so you could be fairly extroverted and outgoing. You like expensive things and you're prepared to work hard to make sure you get them. You're warm and loving.

Virgo With the Moon in the same sign as the Sun, you'll find that your Virgo character is doubly strong. So, you're likely to work harder, be more critical and worry more than most. But you're also likely to be wittier, more practical and more helpful, too.

Libra Virgos are known for their neat habits and Libra is a sign that's characterized by a sense of elegance and refinement. Put these together, then, and you'll see why you have such a strong eye for beauty, harmony and art.

Scorpio There's a good deal more to you than meets the eye! You may appear cool and composed on the surface but you're steamy and passionate underneath. When you've got your teeth into a project, you won't give up until you've finished.

Sagittarius You can be quite a wise little philosopher in your own way and your friends will come and pour out their troubles to you or ask you for your advice when they have problems. You like to help others, so you will always make time to listen.

Capricorn You really take yourself and your work very seriously indeed and people know they can rely on you.

You have what is known as 'an old head on young shoulders'. It wouldn't hurt to mellow out and have some fun, you know.

Aquarius You're so tender-hearted, you'll do anything to help sick animals, children in need or anyone less fortunate than yourself. You believe in making the world a better place for everyone and everything to live in.

Pisces Kind, compassionate and sensitive, you love helping others. You're an interesting mixture of practical know-how and artistic inspiration. You could be a natural healer, so think about a career as a nurse, doctor or vet.

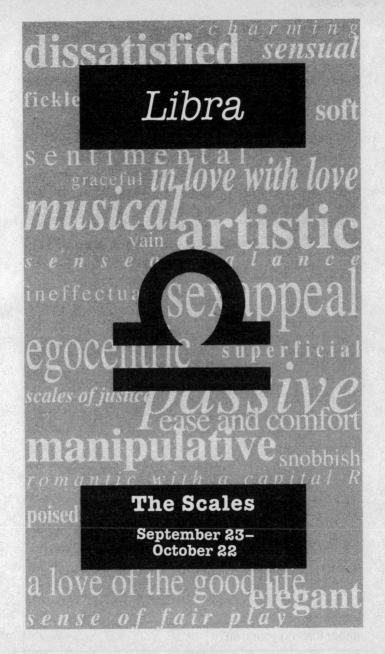

charming sensual

dissatisfied

fickle

Libra

soft

sentimental

graceful *in love with love*

musical artistic

vain

sense balance

ineffectual sex appeal

egocentric superficial

scales of justice passive

ease and comfort

manipulative snobbish

romantic with a capital R

poised

The Scales

September 23– October 22

a love of the good life elegant

sense of fair play

Are You A True Libran?

Find out how typical you are of your sign. Check only **one** box for each question.

	Often	Sometimes	Never
Are you rather dreamy?	◯	◯	◯
Do you procrastinate – put things off until another day?	◯	◯	◯
Do you find that your environment tends to influence your mood (e.g. being in a seedy part of town makes you depressed)?	◯	◯	◯
Are you a good listener?	◯	◯	◯
Do you go along with others just to keep the peace?	◯	◯	◯
Do you hate drama or films about squalid living conditions?	◯	◯	◯
Do you find it difficult to make up your mind?	◯	◯	◯
Do you prefer working with another person rather than on your own?	◯	◯	◯

	Often	Sometimes	Never
Do you find you have to borrow money in order to afford the things you want?	◯	◯	◯
Does having a row with someone make you ill?	◯	◯	◯
Are you a bit of a snob?	◯	◯	◯
Do you often dream of being a super model or a rock star?	◯	◯	◯

Score: You score 2 points for an "Often" answer, 1 point for a "Sometimes" answer, 0 points for a "Never."

0 - 12 You're not a typical Libran, so perhaps you were born at the very beginning or at the very end of your sign, which would modify your character. If so, you're what is known as "cuspal" and are a mixture of two signs. If you were born at the very beginning of Libra, you share some of Virgo's characteristics and should read up on that sign too. If you were born at the end, you share some of Scorpio's characteristics, so read about that sign as well.

13 - 18 Although you do have many Libran characteristics, your Moon placement probably modifies your character and personality quite noticeably. Find out more by reading about how the Moon affects your emotions on page 102.

19 and Over You're a true Libran. Now read on and find out more about yourself.

Sign Associations

- **Element** – Air
- **Lucky day** – Friday
- **Lucky number** – 6
- **Stone** – Opal
- **Flower** – Rose
- **Color** – Lavender
- **Libra rules** – The veins and the kidneys

Your Ruling Planet

As a Libran, your ruling planet is Venus and so you may be interested in some of the things that are associated with this planet. The symbol for Venus is:

Venus is associated with:

- *a love of art, music and drama*
- *social graces and good manners*
- *love and lovers*
- *interest in fashion and beauty*
- *food and catering*
- *floristry*

★ **Famous people who share your sign** ★

Brett Anderson, Bob Geldof, Chris Lowe, Michael Douglas, Roger Moore, Christopher Reeve, Anneka Rice, Dawn French, Danni Minogue, Sting

Keynotes to Libra

you belong to the Air element, so: you're chatty and sociable. You're also idealistic, particularly about people. Beauty is important to you.

your talents and interests lie in: the ability to give impartial advice, to judge and weigh up different opinions, tact, diplomacy and discretion, mediating, peace-keeping, design and architecture, art, sculpture, music, dance, sales, socializing.

you work: better in company or as part of a team.

you hate: being snubbed by anyone.

at school: you're especially good at creative subjects such as design or music. Poetry and drama, too, will appeal to your romantic nature. Because you hate roughness of any sort, you'd find it hard to thrive in a very tough environment and, ideally, you'd do a great deal better in a school set in pleasant surroundings. As long as you've got at least one best friend you'll be happy and settled. But if that close friend should leave for any reason, you'd be very upset and lost until you found someone else on your wave length to take his or her place.

you spend your money: on good quality things. You hate cheap, shoddy stuff so you'll always buy the best gear you can afford. Music tapes or CDs are always favorites.

you like your bedroom to be: sumptuous and preferably light and airy. If it's dark and dreary or doesn't have a decent view, you would find it uncomfortable and difficult to concentrate or do your homework in it properly. It's surprising what a lovely view can do for your inspiration. Because you're so creative, your room will be pretty and arty.

You keep fit by: doing ballet, Yoga or T'ai Chi. A game of tennis with a friend or a gentle stroll – nothing too energetic, mind – are typical activities for you.

♎ ♎ ♎

The Libran Personality

Librans have expensive tastes. You can tell by their clothes and by the things they own. Ideally, they would like everything in their lives to be beautiful. In fact, anything vulgar, dirty, sordid or sleazy really turns them off. And because they're fundamentally lazy, they want everything to fall into their laps. They want life to be cushy. So the problem is, when they do come across anything in life that they consider gross or messy or disgusting, instead of getting up and doing something about it, they develop the habit of simply shutting their eyes to the problem.

For example, they simply refuse to notice the piles of dirty laundry heaped in the corner of their bedroom, or the stack of empty coffee cups where the dregs are slowly turning green with mold! Out of sight, for a Libran, is definitely out of mind!

Image is incredibly important to them and they do everything in style. "Suave" and "panache" are words that are often used to describe people born in Libra. They take great pride in their appearance and they'll spend ages getting their hair just right, making sure their socks match their shoes or that their shirt collar doesn't turn up at the points. They may be late for school, but they'll arrive perfectly dressed and coiffured.

Just as they like everything in their lives to be lovely and balanced, so they also like everything to be peaceful. Arguments, for example, make them ill. They so dislike bad feelings or letting people down that they'll do anything so as not to fall out with their friends. That's why Librans are so often accused of being "yes people."

Sounds familiar? Go on, come clean!

What you really think about yourself but wouldn't dream of saying to anyone else: *Hey! I'm the coolest dude/chick in the world!*

What you want most in the world: *The good life (i.e. laze about all day long and have everyone else running around after you!)*

What your mom would say to you: *Look! I haven't had the time to wash your blue shirt. You'll just have to make do with the pink one, instead!*

What your teacher would write in your school report: *Nice manners.*

What your best friend would say to you: *Go and sort out those two over there, will you, and make them see sense before one of them gets hurt.*

How to insult a Libran: *Buzz off, you self-satisfied, snobbish wimp!*

If your boyfriend is a typical Libran...

You can spot him a mile away because he's: great looking. He's likely to be on the tall side, fairly thin and with straight, shiny hair – and no matter what he does to it, it always seems to fall in a center part. His nose is what you might describe as Grecian or aqualine and his mouth is kissable because it's sooooo gorgeous! Though he may be wearing casual clothes, there's something very stylish about him. You can tell he's got great taste. Everything will be matching and everything will be in the right place. He may not be the most hunky guy in the world, but he's definitely the most swoonsome.

- **He likes:** *beautiful women.*

- **He needs:** *a loving relationship.*

- **He's great because he's:** *so cool.*

- **He's a drag because he's:** *so smug.*

- **Never:** *create a scene when you're together in public.*

On your first date with him: this is one romantic dude and you can be sure this date will put stars in your eyes! He'll be charming, gentle and good-mannered (he does rather fancy himself as Sir Galahad, you see). Whether you spend the time together listening to music, going to the movies or just walking hand-in-hand in the park, this is one dream-boat you won't forget in a hurry.

On his birthday, spoil him: with a new set of strings for his guitar.

If your girlfriend is a typical Libran...

You can spot her a mile away because she's: a babe. She's got a lovely heart-shaped face with large shiny eyes, a pretty cupid-bow mouth and when she laughs you can see her teeth which are white and even. You can easily pick her out of a crowd because she'll be the ultra-feminine one with her soft skin and silky hair. It won't matter what she's wearing because she'd look good even in an old sack – she just has that knack of looking great and turning out right. She's the sort who could go through a hedge backwards and still come out without a hair out of place.

- **She likes:** *anything pretty, feminine – and very expensive.*

- **She needs:** *a hunky guy to take care of her.*

- **She's great because she's:** *so sweet.*

- **She's a drag because she:** *is full of herself.*

- **Never:** *take her anywhere sleazy.*

On your first date with her: she'll expect you to turn up looking very elegant. She goes for the mature type who looks expensive and has plenty of savvy. Giving her a little posy of flowers that she could pin to her lapel would make her eyes shine. She's so charming and easy and relaxing to be with that you'll find this one of the most pleasant dates you've ever had.

On her birthday, spoil her: by giving her an expensive box of watercolors and the best sketch pad you can find.

Libra in love

♥ **You have a special understanding with:**
Geminis, Aquarians and, of course, other Librans.

♥ **In a relationship your best qualities are:**
charming manners, good listener, good conversationalist.

♥ **In a relationship your worst qualities are:**
laziness, inability to make up your mind, a roving eye.

♥ **Your ideal partner:** someone who's sweet, soft
and gentle – a pretty girl or a handsome guy, with artistic
or musical talents. Anyone aggressive or domineering
would just make your life hell.

Dos & don'ts for happy relationships

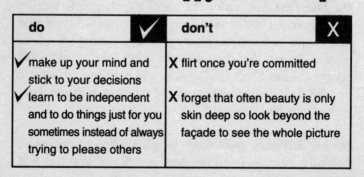

do ✓	don't X
✓ make up your mind and stick to your decisions	X flirt once you're committed
✓ learn to be independent and to do things just for you sometimes instead of always trying to please others	X forget that often beauty is only skin deep so look beyond the façade to see the whole picture

Your Libra love chart

Libra with	♥ Your relationship together ♥	At a glance
Aries	attraction of opposites?	♥♥♥
Taurus	a class act	♥♥♥
Gemini	choice	♥♥♥♥♥
Cancer	soggy	♥♥
Leo	expect difficulties	♥
Virgo	heavy weather	♥
Libra	shall we, shan't we…	♥♥♥
Scorpio	worth a try	♥♥♥
Sagittarius	easy come, easy go	♥♥
Capricorn	no, no, no, no, no!	♥
Aquarius	out of sight!	♥♥♥♥♥
Pisces	tender and true	♥♥♥♥

♥ = grim   ♥♥ = so-so   ♥♥♥ = stick with it

♥♥♥♥ = magnetic   ♥♥♥♥♥ = fwoarrrgh!

The Moon and Your Emotions

Everything you've read about yourself so far has been
based on the Sun's position at the time of your birth which,
in your case, was in the sign of Libra. This tells you a great
deal about your character. But if you want to know more
about your emotions, you need to know in which sign the
Moon was placed when you were born.

Find your Moon sign by turning to the tables on page 187
then read below how it works with your Sun sign to affect
and modify your Libran Nature.

Sun in Libra with Moon in:

Aries You've got tons of energy which means you're not
quite as laid-back as other Librans. Impatience can sometimes get the better of you and you may leave projects
half-done. You're a true adventurer – especially in love.

Taurus You're soft and sensual and simply adore luxury.
Life has to be fun and you're going to enjoy yourself come
what may. You're prepared to work hard, though, to ensure
you get nice things and a cushy life. You've got lots of
talents and you're highly creative.

Gemini Can you talk or can you talk? You're clever and
imaginative and you take an interest in everything that's
going on around you. You have loads of hobbies but may
only skim the surface of each one. You have ants in your
pants.

Cancer You're a kind, gracious and caring person who
loves making everything nice for everyone. It's very
important for you to have a close buddy to work with and

who can share your ideas as well as your problems.

Leo Fairy tales are filled with beautiful people like you. You're dreamy and romantic but also vivacious and theatrical. You have great taste and want the best in everything – including the best looker in town!

Virgo You have a sweet, charming nature coupled with a good brain. You're always prepared to help others so long as it doesn't involve messy work – you can't stand anything to do with blood and gore.

Libra You dither and dawdle, you um and ah, and still end up sitting on the fence! You are an absolute dreamboat who tends, more often than not, to be living in a dream world. You have terrific ideas and lots of talent – apply them.

Scorpio You positively ooze sex appeal. You're cool on the surface but deep, deep inside, smoldering with intense emotions. You have a good analytical brain and love working things out.

Sagittarius A brilliant negotiator, full of tact and diplomacy. Everyone trusts you and respects your judgement and when your friends have fallen out, you come along like the cavalry and get things sorted out.

Capricorn You're an excellent judge of character, diplomatic, fair and able to tap into other people's feelings. Success is important to you and because you'd like to be rich and have lots of nice things, you're prepared to work really hard to get to the top. You're choosy about who you hang around with so you can be very picky over your girl/boyfriends.

Aquarius You're a fascinating and interesting mixture. One minute you want everything cool and calm and even, and the next minute you want thrills and excitement and feel compelled to make waves. You're clever and you have a terrific imagination.

Pisces You're very laid-back and easy going. You need romance in your life so you tend to be idealistic and to see life through rose-colored glasses. You like to believe the best about everyone. Highly creative, you're one of life's born artists.

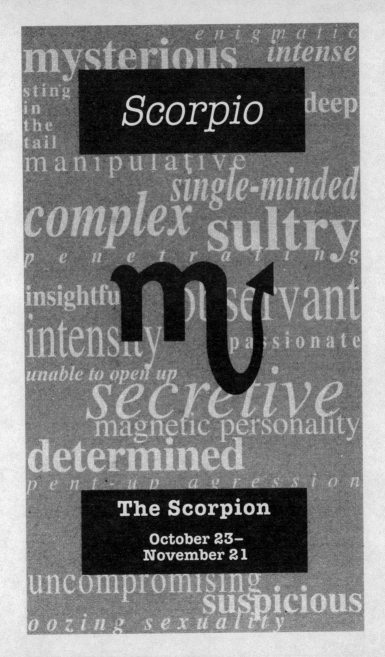

enigmatic

mysterious   intense

sting
in
the
tail   deep

Scorpio

manipulative

single-minded

complex   sultry

penetrating

insightful   observant

intensity   passionate

unable to open up

secretive

magnetic personality

determined

pent-up agression

The Scorpion

October 23–
November 21

uncompromising

suspicious

oozing sexuality

Are You A True Scorpio?

Find out how typical you are of your sign. Check only **one** box for each question.

	Often	Sometimes	Never
Are you a fan of mysteries and whodunnits?	⊗	○	○
Do you bear grudges?	○	⊗	○
Do you bottle up your emotions?	⊙	⊗	○
Are you generally lucky?	⊗	⊙	○
Do you have a lot of pent-up energy?	○	⊙	⊗
Do you never forget a slight?	⊗	○	○
Do you take everything very seriously?	○	⊗	○
Do you like keeping secrets?	⊗	○	○
Do you get deeply involved with people?	⊙	○	⊗
Do you get jealous easily?	○	⊙	⊗

	Often	Sometimes	Never
If someone has upset you, do you spend a long time planning how to get even with them?	⊘	⊙	◯
Do you often dream that you're a femme fatale (if you're female) or magnetically desirable (if you're male)?	⊛	◯	⊘

Score: You score 2 points for an "Often" answer, 1 point for a "Sometimes" answer, 0 points for a "Never."

0 - 12 You're not a typical Scorpio, so perhaps you were born at the very beginning or at the very end of your sign, which would modify your character. If so, you're what is known as "cuspal" and are a mixture of two signs. If you were born at the very beginning of Scorpio, you share some Libran characteristics and should read about that sign as well. If you were born at the end, you share some Sagittarian characteristics, so read up on that sign too.

13 - 18 Although you do have many Scorpio characteristics, your Moon placement probably modifies your character and personality quite noticeably. Find out more by reading about how the Moon affects your emotions on page 116.

19 and Over You're a true Scorpio. Now read on and find out more about yourself.

Sign Associations

- **Element** – Water
- **Lucky day** – Tuesday
- **Lucky number** – 8
- **Stone** – Topaz, Jasper
- **Flower** – Chrysanthemum
- **Color** – Claret, magenta
- **Scorpio rules** – The reproductive system

Your Ruling Planet

As a Scorpio, your ruling planet is Pluto so you may be interested in some of the things that are associated with this planet. The symbol for Pluto is:

Pluto is associated with:

- *the underworld*
- *mines, caves and underground caverns*
- *taxes, legacies, insurances*
- *undercover activity, e.g. spying and detection*
- *sex and the sexual organs*
- *regeneration and transformation – life, death and rebirth*

★ **Famous people who share your sign** ★

Clint Eastwood, Julia Roberts, Winona Ryder, Ant McPartlin, Bryan Adams, Prince Charles, Letitia Dean, Griff Rhys-Jones, Jonathan Ross, Frank Bruno

Keynotes to Scorpio

you belong to the Water element, so: you're sensitive, emotionally intense and your heart often rules your head. You enjoy being near water.

your talents and interests lie in: detective work, super sleuthing, crosswords, puzzles, uncovering mysteries, criminal detection, psychology, anything gory, ghosts, ghouls and other spooky things, medicine, chemicals, poisons, forensics, photography, magic and conjuring tricks, the stage.

you work: single-mindedly.

you hate: being taunted.

at school: Scorpios are very black or white in their opinions, so you either love school or you hate it. If you like school and the work you have to do, you'll make great progress and achieve brilliant results. You're particularly good at things like biology and chemistry, anything investigative that needs research or digging around for facts. If, however, you dislike school, you're likely to misbehave badly and slack off whenever you can.

you spend your money: on CDs (probably heavy metal), crime and horror novels.

you like your bedroom to be: dramatic and exciting (and a bit theatrically dangerous-looking too), so you may want to paint everything red and black.

you keep fit by: working out and playing a lot of sports. You have tons of energy and it's important for you to channel it in the right direction, so sports are ideal for you – not only now when you're young, but also throughout your life.

♏ ♏ ♏

The Scorpio Personality

It's not by mere chance that people born between October 23 and November 21 are represented by the scorpion. If you know a thing or two about scorpions, you'll know that they're dangerous creatures. They're okay so long as they're left to their own devices but if you stir them up, poke them around a bit or otherwise disturb them when they don't want to be disturbed, they'll whip their tails round and jab you with their poisonous sting. When it comes to their enemies, they show no mercy. They're vicious and ruthless, and they attack to kill.

That may sound a bit extreme, but even the most ardent insect-lover would agree that when it comes to scorpions, it pays to respect them!

Now, as far as Scorpio-born individuals go, they too have a sting in their tails – although an invisible one, of course. Upset one of them and you'll soon find out. They'll lash out at you with a few well chosen words that don't half hit the spot!

On the positive side, these individuals are fascinating. The guys tend to be dark and brooding and the girls are sultry exotics. Passion is their middle name and they simply ooze sex appeal.

Love them or hate them, Scorpios are deep, powerful,

mysterious individuals, whom you simply can't ignore. If you're a Scorpio, do you think this description rings true?

What you really think about yourself but wouldn't dream of saying to anyone else: *I'm so street-wise.*

What you want most in the world: *To be powerful.*

What your mom would say to you: *Stop staring at me like that. Are you trying to hypnotize me or something?*

What your teacher would write in your school report: *Shows remarkable powers of concentration.*

What your best friend would say to you: *You're the one person I can trust because I know you will never, ever divulge a secret.*

How to insult a Scorpio: *You really think you're hot, don't you, you feeble dork?*

If your boyfriend is a typical Scorpio...

You can spot him a mile away because he's: dark and mysterious looking – mainly because he has dark eyes and dark curly hair and he likes dark clothes. He may even be wearing a leather jacket (he favors the bad boy/tough guy image). All this gives him an unmistakably brooding look and he's probably the one with a frown on his face. Or he could be wearing black shades – just for that air of cool mystique they give him. He has strong facial features, with good bone structure and a body rippling with well-developed muscles. Make no mistake, sister, this is one hot guy!

- **He likes:** *to act tough.*

- **He needs:** *to let off steam.*

- **He's great because he'll:** *never kiss and tell.*

- **He's a drag because he:** *comes on too strong.*

- **Never:** *make him the slightest bit jealous.*

On your first date with him: the thing you'll notice most is that you're the center of his attention. He'll look deep into your eyes with an amazing gaze – Svengali had nothing on this guy! It might be a bit uncomfortable at first but stare right back into his – he'll enjoy the challenge. He's a bit of an unknown entity, this one, and you'll need a good deal more than one date to figure him out. He may be looking for a conquest so you should consider carefully whether you want to be just another one of his statistics.

On his birthday, spoil him: by taking him to see *Terminator*.

If your girlfriend is a typical Scorpio...

You can spot her a mile away because she's: a really lovely chick with dark, glossy hair and eyes that are heavily made up. There's definitely something exotic and stunning about this girl. Perhaps it's her dress sense or perhaps it's the way she moves, rather slinky and dead sexy. Whatever it is, you won't have any trouble picking her out because she's one helluva gorgeous gal.

- **She likes:** *to be in control.*

- **She needs:** *your undivided attention.*

- **She's great because she's:** *deeply loving.*

- **She's a drag because she's:** *mean with jealousy.*

- **Never:** *toy with her affections (if you know what's good for you!)*

On your first date with her: you may feel as if she's measuring you up. She'll be very curious and will worm out everything there is to know about you, but she won't be giving much about herself away. She's an absolutely fascinating creature and you're bound to have an exciting date with her. Beware of her famous jealousy, though, and whatever you do, don't eye up any other talent when you're in her company. Take her to a movie full of passion and intrigue. She'll adore the film and the dark intimacy too!

On her birthday, spoil her: by giving her a pair of long black gloves.

Scorpio in love

♥ **You have a special understanding with:**
Cancerians, Pisceans and, of course, other Scorpios.

♥ **In a relationship your best qualities are:**
true passion, protectiveness, you never give a secret away.

♥ **In a relationship your worst qualities are:**
secrecy, jealousy, intensity and ruthless sarcasm.

♥ **Your ideal partner:** must be as emotional and passionate as you. Someone who is prepared to stand by you no matter what. S/he will be flattered by your undivided attention and would never dream of flirting with anyone else but you!

Do's & don'ts for happy relationships

do	✓	don't	X
✓ give your partner space		X come on strong because you'll only frighten people off	
✓ relax more		X feel you have to get even all the time	

Your Scorpio love chart

Scorpio with ♥	Your relationship together ♥	At a glance
Aries	competitive but hot	♥♥♥♥
Taurus	attraction of opposites?	♥♥♥
Gemini	superficiality vs intensity = no win	♥
Cancer	dynamite	♥♥♥♥♥
Leo	wow!	♥♥♥♥
Virgo	at odds	♥♥
Libra	give it a try	♥♥♥
Scorpio	watch the sparks fly	♥♥♥♥
Sagittarius	a non-starter	♥
Capricorn	kerpow!	♥♥♥♥
Aquarius	tense or what?	♥
Pisces	the tops!	♥♥♥♥♥

♥ = grim   ♥♥ = so-so   ♥♥♥ = stick with it

♥♥♥♥ = magnetic   ♥♥♥♥♥ = fwoarrrgh!

The Moon and Your Emotions

Everything you've read about yourself so far has been based on the Sun's position at the time of your birth which, in your case, was in the sign of Scorpio. This tells you a great deal about your character. But if you want to know more about your emotions, you need to know in which sign the Moon was placed when you were born.

Find your Moon sign by turning to the tables on page 187 then read below how it works with your Sun sign to affect and modify your Scorpio nature.

Sun in Scorpio with Moon in:

Aries You're strong and fearless and would make a superb athlete. You have tons and tons of energy and a huge need for adventure and excitement. Emotionally, you may find yourself up one minute and down the next.

Taurus The moon in this placement adds even more strength to your character but does tend to stabilize your emotions. When you set your heart on something, you'll go all out until you get it. Beware pig-headedness.

Gemini You're pretty good at figuring people out and reading between the lines. You're quick and clever and you don't miss a trick. You're witty and brilliant at one-liner put-downs. Maybe you'd make a great journalist!

Cancer Both Scorpio and Cancer are Water signs which means lots of emotional sensitivity. With this combination you could be prone to mean n' moody dramas. But you are highly intuitive and you have a special gift with animals.

Leo You're strong and determined, loving, loyal and supportive towards those you care about. Once you've dug your heels in, though, nothing will shift you. You possess a natural animal magnetism which draws people to you.

Virgo You're a deeply caring person who likes to work hard and is possibly drawn to vocational work. Perhaps you might think about a career as a doctor or a vet. You could be extraordinarily tidy and you may find it difficult to talk about your feelings.

Libra You're some dish! You like mixing with others and don't mind getting involved in social chit-chat. Your expensive tastes can make you a bit of a snob, though, and you dream of living life the five-star way.

Scorpio With this combination, you're probably the strongest type of Scorpio there is. This means you're deep and determined, passionate and persistent, sultry and sexy, secretive and suspicious. You are one powerful person!

Sagittarius Most Scorpios take themselves too seriously but with the Moon in Sagittarius you're blessed with a sense of humor and that helps to lighten the load. You're idealistic and interested in justice so a career in law would suit you.

Capricorn You have huge drive and immense will-power. You're as strong as an ox and just about as immovable. You know what you want and you work your socks off until you reach your goal. Hey! Ease up a bit.

Aquarius Your animal magnetism attracts people to you, yet you want to be free and independent. Your heart wants commitment but you can be intolerant of others.

You're brilliant at reading people and could make a terrific psychoanalyst.

Pisces With both your Sun and Moon in Water signs your emotions will be intense. You are very sensitive and will feel everything everyone else around you is feeling. This makes you sympathetic and shrewd.

Sagittarius

optimistic
impatient expansive
selfish
belief open
in
justice
extoverted
visionary outward-looking
honest naive
happy-go-lucky
sympathetic
idealist intuitive
fortunes
hopeful
all's well that ends well
generous
distant horizons
enthusiastic trusting
full of the joys of spring
blunt
rash
never say die
philosophical
hope springs eternal

The Archer

November 22–
December 21

Are You A True Sagittarian?

Find out how typical you are of your sign. Check only **one** box for each question.

	Often	Sometimes	Never
Does the thought of being in jail or in any way losing your freedom terrify you?	○	○	○
Do you like going on long journeys?	○	○	○
Do you go horseback riding? If not, do you think you'd like to?	○	○	○
Do you trust people?	○	○	○
Do you like exercising/playing sports?	○	○	○
Do you go to the library?	○	○	○
Do you generally expect things to work out all right?	○	○	○
Do your hunches pay off, i.e. do you think you're intuitive?	○	○	○
Do you prefer to be outside rather than indoors?	○	○	○

	Often	Sometimes	Never
Are you lucky?	◯	◯	◯
Do you find your tactlessness embarrasses people?	◯	◯	◯
Do boys (if you're female), or girls (if you're male), think you're flirting with them when you're only trying to be friendly?	◯	◯	◯

Score: You score 2 points for an "Often" answer, 1 point for a "Sometimes" answer, 0 points for a "Never."

0 - 12 You're not a typical Sagittarian, so perhaps you were born at the very beginning or at the very end of your sign, which would modify your character. If so, you're what is known as "cuspal" and are a mixture of two signs. If you were born at the very beginning of Sagittarius, you share some of Scorpio's characteristics and should read about that sign as well. If you were born at the end, you share some of Capricorn's characteristics, so read up on that sign too.

13 - 18 Although you do have many Sagittarian characteristics, your Moon placement probably modifies your character and personality quite noticeably. Find out more by reading about how the Moon affects your emotions on page 130.

19 and Over You're a true Sagittarian. Now read on and find out more about yourself.

Sign Associations

- **Element** – Fire
- **Lucky day** – Thursday
- **Lucky number** – 9
- **Stone** – Turquoise
- **Flower** – Narcissus
- **Color** – Purple, violet, indigo
- **Sagittarius rules** – The hips and thighs

Your Ruling Planet

As a Sagittarian, your ruling planet is Jupiter so you may be interested in some of the things that are associated with this planet. The symbol for Jupiter is:

Jupiter is associated with:

- *publishing, religion, politics and the law*
- *schools and higher education*
- *luck, good fortune, risks and gambling*
- *philosophy, morals and ideals*
- *travel and foreign languages*
- *hunting and sport*
- *food and drink*

★ **Famous people who share your sign** ★

Ian Botham, Mel Smith, Steven Spielberg, Kristian Schmidt, Toby Anstis, Ronnie Corbett, Gary Lineker, Kim Basinger, Judi Dench, Tina Turner, Jeff Bridges, Brad Pitt, Ryan Giggs

Keynotes to Sagittarius

*you belong to the **Fire** element, so:* you're enthusiastic, warm, open, generous and friendly. You're noisy and extroverted.

*your **talents** and **interests** lie in:* working with animals, sports, publishing, travel, foreign languages, the legal profession, nursing, alternative religions.

*you **work:*** by putting everything off, then having to work like blazes at the last minute.

*you **hate:*** being tied down.

*at **school:*** you're well suited to school life since Sagittarius rules learning and education. On the whole, you're likely to enjoy your lessons, although sometimes you tend to stare out of the window wistfully, wondering what's going on in the blue yonder while here you are stuck in the classroom. But you do love getting out on to the sports field and you adore trips to exhibitions and museums – well, apart from getting out of math and getting into the fresh air, trips out mean travel and different things to see and do. Because of your love of learning, you're very likely to want to go on to college.

*you spend your **money:*** in an easy-come, easy-go fashion because you know you're lucky and you've discovered that money comes to you somehow or other when you need it. You're extremely generous and tend to give your money away to those you think need it more than you do.

*you like your **bedroom** to be:* warm and cozy

with a definite lived-in look – which probably means messy, very messy. Besides, how can anyone feel comfortable in a room that's all clean and tidy? So there'll be books and magazines and dirty socks way deep on the floor but, hey! that's what makes you feel at home, so who's complaining?

you keep fit by: playing plenty of sports. Your sign rules games so you're likely to enjoy physical education. However, you're probably happier in team games, or in contact sports, than working out on your own.

The Sagittarian Personality

Sagittarians are the freewheelers of the Zodiac, happy, easy-going, laid-back people with a very casual attitude to everything they do. Perhaps it's their cheerfulness, or their take-it-or-leave-it approach to things, or the fact that they're extraordinarily lucky. Whatever it is, they just don't get fazed like other people.

Freedom, though, is all-important. They love to think they could roam the wide open spaces all day long. They're always thinking of distant horizons and of what could be over the brow of the next hill.

That's what makes them so adventurous and optimistic. They're excited about the future and they're always looking forward, hoping something better will turn up. And, surprise, surprise! For Sagittarians, something usually does.

These people are open and honest and sincere – sometimes

too honest for their own good. Because they have a tendency to say the wrong thing at the wrong time, they can make horrendously embarrassing gaffs. Being outspoken is all very well but there are times when you need to pick your words delicately. Sagittarians aren't very good at treading on eggshells and are even worse when it comes to buttoning their lip! As far as they're concerned, what-you-see-is-what-you-get. No pretensions, no complications, no whitewash. Take it or leave it!

If you're a what-you-see-is-what-you-get Sagittarian, how does this square up with you?

What you really think about yourself but wouldn't dream of saying to anyone else: *I haven't got time to waste hanging around here.*

What you want most in the world: *To experience everything, at least once.*

What your mom would say to you: *I wish you'd come home on time, for a change.*

What your teacher would write in your school report: *Good work but needs to sustain concentration.*

What your best friend would say to you: *You lucky duck, you won the lottery again. Next time buy a ticket for me, will you?*

How to insult a Sagittarian: *Anyone with a mouth as big as yours should learn to keep it shut, dork!*

If your boyfriend is a typical Sagittarian...

You can spot him a mile away because he's: tallish and athletic with an out-doorsy look. He's got shiny, smiling eyes and probably a wide grin on his face. Look for the guy who's wearing the most comfortable looking clothes – Sagittarian guys can't abide fussing over their clothes, and hate dressing up like a dog's dinner. If he's wearing a track suit it's probably got a sporty emblem on it, or look for a badge that tells you which sports club he belongs to.

- **He likes:** *having lots of strings to his bow.*

- **He needs:** *a faithful dog who'll go everywhere with him.*

- **He's great because he's:** *always cheerful.*

- **He's a drag because he's:** *so untidy.*

- **Never:** *fence him in.*

On your first date with him: don't expect to go anywhere too fancy, he's not that kind of guy. He hates formal occasions when he has to dress up all stiff and starchy – but if he has to he will, and he'll turn out great. He's funny and he'll make you laugh, but he can also be quite blunt and you'll have to develop a thick skin. Don't worry, he doesn't mean it, he wouldn't dream of offending anyone. You might go bowling or skating but whatever it is you do, you'll have fun.

On his birthday, spoil him: by taking him to an adventure park – and letting him loose.

If your girlfriend is a typical Sagittarian...

You can spot her a mile away because she's: the one who's tossing her head up like a young colt. There's a very open and friendly look on her face, and because she's usually so cheerful, she'll probably be smiling or, more often than not, laughing loudly. She looks quite relaxed and may be wearing loose, sporty sort of clothes: she can't stand anything tight and restricting. And though she'll look terrific in jeans, since her sign rules the hips, she may be just a tad broad in the rear.

- **She likes:** *to be treated like one of the guys.*

- **She needs:** *you to be the big brother she always wanted.*

- **She's great because she's:** *totally honest.*

- **She's a drag because she's:** *always saying the wrong thing.*

- **Never:** *try to clip her wings.*

On your first date with her: she'll take your breath away with her bluntness. She doesn't mind telling you the most intimate details about herself, often laughing at her own faults and mistakes and making you laugh about them too. But she will expect you to be honest and candid back. This is likely to be one of the most relaxing dates you've ever had because she won't make waves and will enjoy whatever it is you've lined up.

On her birthday, spoil her: by treating her to a horse-back riding lesson.

Sagittarius in love

♥ **You have a special understanding with:**
Aries, Leos and, of course, other Sagittarians.

♥ **In a relationship your best qualities are:**
total trust, ability to relax, great fun to be with.

♥ **In a relationship your worst qualities are:**
lack of diplomacy, need for freedom, too casual by half.

♥ **Your ideal partner:** is someone who's easy-going like you and shares your love of the outdoor life. Someone who won't insist you dress up all the time and who won't complain about the mud you walk through the house. Or who doesn't mind about camping in the rain and actually prefers wearing jeans and sneakers most of the time. And who's mad about picnics – even in the dead of winter.

Dos & don'ts for happy relationships

do ✔	don't ✗
✔ think before you speak	✗ ever lose your sense of humor
✔ learn to say "no"	✗ be so trusting all the time

Your Sagittarius love chart

Sagittarius with ♥ Your relationship together ♥ At a glance

Aries	hot stuff!	♥♥♥♥♥
Taurus	like old pudding	♥♥
Gemini	attraction of opposites?	♥♥♥
Cancer	some comforts	♥♥
Leo	we're talking body heat here!	♥♥♥♥♥
Virgo	sad	♥
Libra	warmed-up sludge	♥♥
Scorpio	stormy weather	♥
Sagittarius	action stations	♥♥♥♥♥
Capricorn	in your dreams	♥
Aquarius	has its moments	♥♥♥
Pisces	like walking over quick-sand	♥

♥ = grim   ♥♥ = so-so   ♥♥♥ = stick with it

♥♥♥♥ = magnetic   ♥♥♥♥♥ = fwoarrrgh!

The Moon and Your Emotions

Everything you've read about yourself so far has been based on the Sun's position at the time of your birth which, in your case, was in the sign of Sagittarius. This tells you a great deal about your character. But if you want to know more about your emotions, you need to know in which sign the Moon was placed when you were born.

Find your Moon sign by turning to the tables on page 187 then read below how it works with your Sun sign to affect and modify your Sagittarian nature.

Sun in Sagittarius with Moon in:

Aries You certainly don't let the grass grow under your feet. You're excitable and adventurous and you tend to take on whatever grabs your imagination. However, you may not have the patience to see it through to the end. Be tactful.

Taurus You're kind and always ready to help those in need. You're probably highly talented and creative in lots of ways and you like an easy, comfortable and cushy life. The Moon in Taurus makes you calmer, steadier and more practical.

Gemini Have you got itchy feet, or what? You're sharp, clever, bright as a button but you can't sit still for a minute. You're probably brilliant at English and foreign languages. Try joining the debating society or drama group.

Cancer You may find it hard to make up your mind whether you prefer to be out-and-about independent or attached-to-your-nest home-bird. You're kind and sensitive and intuitive. Mood swings can sometimes get the better of you, though.

Leo You're a bundle of fun. Dramatic, extroverted, outgoing, the world is your oyster. Although you could be a little loud sometimes, you do bring sunshine into people's lives. Think about going into show biz. But beware vanity.

Virgo More careful than the average Sagittarian, since a Virgo Moon can help to peg you down. You have great ideas as well as practical know-how. You could become a fine teacher, doctor or vet. Working with computers would also suit.

Libra A wide circle of friends is crucial for you because you love being with people and talking to others. You're an unusual Sagittarian because you like to look smart and elegant, so dressing up is a delight rather than a pain in the rear.

Scorpio Sagittarians are usually happy-go-lucky types but this Moon placement makes you deep and emotional. You adore investigating things and delving into mysteries. A career as a police surgeon, a detective or lawyer would suit you.

Sagittarius You live for the open spaces and probably thrive on sport. You find being on the move terribly exciting, and a life as a nomad seems very attractive to you. Why don't you start saving now for that round-the-world-trip you're dying to make?

Capricorn Success is important to you so you don't mind putting in lots of extra time to get your work done. Once you start a project you generally see it through to the end. Because you're so kind, you work for good causes and give money to charity.

Aquarius You're certainly far-sighted. This means you often have inspirational ideas that are far ahead of your time. But your friends may think you're a bit off the wall. Hang on to those ideas, though, they could make you a fortune in the future!

Pisces Your Sun is Fire, your Moon is Water. Fire and water make steam, and steam can drive an engine. If you constructively channel your ideas you can make them work, but don't let watery emotions put out your fiery drive.

Capricorn

patient vulnerable
ambitious
steady shy
down
to brave
earth
economical
entertainin business-minded
serious
hard-working feisty
organized
disciplined confident
independent determined
good with money
persistent
solitary strong-willed
introspective shrewd
getting down to brass tacks
caring
tough
fiercely loyal modest
cautious
head for business

The Goat

December 22– January 19

0 = Jenni

Are You A True Capricorn?

Find out how typical you are of your sign. Check only **one** box for each question.

	Often	Sometimes	Never
Do you find it difficult to talk about your feelings?	◯	◯	◯
Do you like being alone?	◯	◯	◯
Is it difficult to relax and let your hair down?	◯	◯	◯
Are you good at saving your money?	◯	◯	◯
Do you work harder than most other people you know?	◯	◯	◯
Do you admire people who are successful?	◯	◯	◯
Do you prefer to hang out with older kids?	◯	◯	◯
Are you especially respectful to your elders?	◯	◯	◯
Do people think you're older than you really are?	◯	◯	◯

	Often	Sometimes	Never
Do you like a steady routine?	○	○	○
If someone asks you out, do you check on how much homework you've got to do first?	○	○	○
Do you dream about being rich and living in a big house with servants?	○	○	○

Score: You score 2 points for an "Often" answer, 1 point for a "Sometimes" answer, 0 points for a "Never."

0 - 12 You're not a typical Capricorn, so perhaps you were born at the very beginning or at the very end of your sign, which would modify your character. If so, you're what is known as "cuspal" and are a mixture of two signs. If you were born at the very beginning of Capricorn, you share some Sagittarian characteristics and should read about that sign as well. If you were born at the end, you share some Aquarian characteristics, so read up on that sign too.

13 - 18 Although you do have many Capricorn characteristics, your Moon placement probably modifies your character and personality quite noticeably. Find out more by reading about how the Moon affects your emotions on page 144.

19 and Over You're a true Capricorn. Now read on and find out more about yourself.

Sign Associations

- **Element** – Earth
- **Lucky day** – Saturday
- **Lucky number** – 7
- **Stone** – Garnet, Onyx
- **Flower** – Carnation
- **Color** – Mid-green
- **Capricorn rules** – The knees and bones

Your Ruling Planet

As a Capricorn, your ruling planet is Saturn so you may be interested in some of the things that are associated with this planet. The symbol for your ruling planet is:

Saturn is associated with:

- *agriculture – reaping, sowing and harvesting*
- *ambition*
- *science and research*
- *banking, economics, savings and thriftiness*
- *learning – the hard way!*
- *limitation and restriction*
- *old age*

★ **Famous people who share your sign** ★

Mel Gibson, Des O'Connor, Rowan Atkinson, David Bowie, Rod Stewart, Noel Edmonds, Annie Lennox, Kate Moss, Kevin Costner, Gary Barlow, David Bellamy

Keynotes to Capricorn

you belong to the Earth element, so: you're practical, logical and down-to-earth. You work hard. You're good with your hands. You have green thumbs.

your talents and interests lie in: anything to do with building or construction, e.g. engineering or architecture, farming, agriculture or horticulture, banking and finance, politics, religions of the world, business and managerial skills, scientific research.

you work: hard! Seriously, steadily and consistently.

you hate: noisy crowds and immature behavior.

at school: you're likely to be respectful and hard-working. Other kids probably think you're a proper little snot who always hands the homework in on time. On the other hand, because you're kind and helpful they know you'll always let them borrow your notes, or spend ages with them at recess explaining theorems or talking them through weather systems for the geography test after lunch. Because you don't play around like the others, teachers always give you the responsible jobs, often picking you out to be the class monitor, for example. The thing you hate is being talked down to. You expect teachers to treat you like an equal, on the same level as themselves. You work better when the lessons are structured and, because you're so good at research, you enjoy project work where you have to dig up facts.

you spend your money: wisely and carefully. You like to see your money grow so you've probably already got lots of it stashed away in the bank.

you like your bedroom to be: tidy and un-cluttered. You have a place for everything and you like everything in its place. You find plain colors, often grays, whites and blacks, much more restful than lots of jazzy razzamatazz all over the place.

you keep fit by: going it alone. That is, because you don't really like team games, you do much better in any kind of solo sport such as running or cycling. In fact, hurdles or long distance would suit you well. And because you're so disciplined, you're more likely to stick to a rigorous training program than any other sign.

$$\text{♑ ♑ ♑}$$

The Capricorn Personality

Complete strangers walk up to Capricorns and say things like: "Cheer up, buddy," or "Never mind, it might never happen." Why? Because Capricorns have a habit of looking miserable even when they're not. They may be filled with the joys of spring, yet people will still take one look at them and say "Keep your chin up, man." This has to be because, for a Capricorn, life is a serious business and this serious attitude tends to be reflected in their faces.

These people are born with an old head on young shoulders. They're sensible and they've had a responsible attitude since they were knee high to a grasshopper. Even as teenagers they behave more like grown-ups than the grown-ups do. They don't go against the teachers, or anyone in authority for that matter, because they believe in respecting their elders and sticking to the rules and regulations.

And another thing about Capricorns is that they never seem to stop working. Whether it's homework or housework, for them it's all work, work, work. Perhaps it's because they're ambitious and determined to get ahead, or possibly because they're perfectionists and like to get a job done well. Whatever it is that drives them on, these people find it hard to simply stop and relax.

In relationships they're quite shy and take a while to make friends. But, once they have chosen their mates, they'll be staunch and loyal and true to them for evermore. A Capricorn friendship is one to cherish.

If you're a Capricorn, are you like this?

What you really think about yourself but wouldn't dream of saying to anyone else: *I'm going to be mega-successful.*

What you want most in the world: *To win the Nobel prize for science.*

What your mom would say to you: *No, sorry, I can't afford $100 for a pair of sneakers for you, just because you want to buy them from the mall!*

What your teacher would write in your school report: *A serious, responsible and thoughtful pupil.*

What your best friend would say to you: *Oh go on, you go and buy the tickets. No one would suspect you're underage.*

How to insult a Capricorn: *No you can't come to my party, you miserable old wet blanket. So shove off.*

If your boyfriend is a typical Capricorn...

You can spot him a mile away because he's: the serious one in the crowd – his face just looks sad most of the time. He's a bit of a stick insect with a long face. A dead give-away are his knobbly knees – but you'll only see them when he's wearing his PE shorts. Otherwise you won't, because he's usually very sensibly dressed, preferring rather bland clothes to funky gear. Your Capricorn boyfriend may not be exactly what you'd call trendy. But he's certainly sensible, reliable and loyal – an altogether thoroughly dependable guy.

- **He likes:** *building things.*

- **He needs:** *someone to help him lighten up.*

- **He's great because he's:** *very organized.*

- **He's a drag because he:** *can be dogmatic, i.e. what he says goes!*

- **Never:** *let him see you squander money.*

On your first date with him: it might be tough going to begin with because he's not the sort who says much about himself. He prefers to talk about things like his work or his collections – Capricorns are notorious collectors! So he may keep his distance at first. But, hang around a bit and you'll soon find that underneath that cool exterior, he's quite a little prankster. Hang around a bit more and his dry, oddball and very unexpected sense of humor will have you holding your sides and rolling in the aisles.

On his birthday, spoil him: by giving him a neat construction kit.

If your girlfriend is a typical Capricorn...

You can spot her a mile away because she's: got such soulful eyes! She may look worried or even sad, although she probably isn't at all. But it'll make you want to cheer her up. She's not very tall but she's fairly slender and ever so smartly dressed. She looks great in simple, classic styles, probably black or dark brown to match her dark eyes. It's fairly certain she won't be wearing anything gaudy or outrageous, though she might be wearing a hat.

- **She likes:** *talking about her school work.*

- **She needs:** *someone to make her laugh.*

- **She's great because she:** *keeps her promises.*

- **She's a drag because she's:** *pessimistic.*

- **Never:** *do anything silly or immature when you're out with her.*

On your first date with her: you may find she's quite shy. She's reserved by nature anyway and tends not to get too close to people too soon. But if she's agreed to go out with you, you should be dancing a jig – she doesn't date just anybody, you know! So you've certainly impressed her to get this far. And though she may appear serious and a bit cool at first, if you're patient you'll discover that she's not quite the cold fish she appears to be. Far from it. When she unwinds, you'll find out just what a hot and feisty babe she really can be.

On her birthday, spoil her: by taking her to a concert – many Capricorns are born musicians.

Capricorn in love

💜 **You have a special understanding with:** Taureans, Virgos and, of course, other Capricorns.

💜 **In a relationship your best qualities are:** loyalty, deep and genuine affection, responsibility, trustworthiness, rock-solid stability. Moreover, you have an excellent memory, so you'll never forget your partner's birthday!

💜 **In a relationship your worst qualities are:** tight-fistedness, emotional coolness, taking things too seriously, bearing grudges.

💜 **Your ideal partner:** is someone who is as strong and dependable as yourself. Someone who will work hard, be loyal and true and who will back you one hundred per cent in achieving your ambitions. A touch of sparkle, and a good sense of humor to pull you out of a slump when necessary, would happily complete the picture.

Dos & don'ts for happy relationships

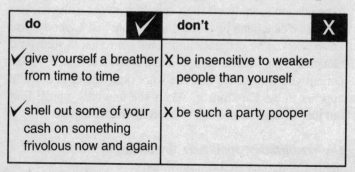

do ✓	don't ✗
✓ give yourself a breather from time to time	✗ be insensitive to weaker people than yourself
✓ shell out some of your cash on something frivolous now and again	✗ be such a party pooper

Your Capricorn love chart

Capricorn with ♥	Your relationship together	♥ At a glance
Aries	powerful	♥♥♥♥
Taurus	choice!	♥♥♥♥♥
Gemini	low-key	♥
Cancer	attraction of opposites?	♥♥♥
Leo	a money-spinner – if it works	♥♥♥
Virgo	mega, mega, mega	♥♥♥♥♥
Libra	odds against	♥
Scorpio	touch of magic	♥♥♥♥
Sagittarius	no hoper	♥
Capricorn	go for it!	♥♥♥♥♥
Aquarius	tough cookie	♥
Pisces	problems, problems, problems	♥♥

♥ = grim   ♥♥ = so-so   ♥♥♥ = stick with it

♥♥♥♥ = magnetic   ♥♥♥♥♥ = fwoarrrgh!

The Moon and Your Emotions

Everything you've read about yourself so far has been based on the Sun's position at the time of your birth which, in your case, was in the sign of Capricorn. This tells you a great deal about your character. But if you want to know more about your emotions, you need to know in which sign the Moon was placed when you were born.

Find your Moon sign by turning to the tables on page 187 then read below how it works with your Sun sign to affect and modify your Capricornian nature.

Sun in Capricorn with Moon in:

Aries Tough, strong and determined, when you put your mind to something, you'll definitely succeed. You're highly competitive and ambitious, and enthusiastic about any new project you take on. Try to be more sensitive to others, though.

Taurus You're a solid, hard-working individual with lots of common sense. You're creative and sensual and you have a good eye for beauty. You like your creature comforts and you need a stable and secure way of life.

Gemini You're a highly intelligent person, good at languages and communications. Although you have a lot of interests, you do, nevertheless, have a talent for being able to organize yourself and your work. So you should do well.

Cancer You're intellectually strong but you're emotionally tender. So this combination will make you more sensitive than most other Capricorns. You love your home and family and you work hard. Try not to worry quite so much.

Leo This combination makes you loving, caring and hard-working. You're a good leader and able to inspire other people with your enthusiasm. Status is important to you and you like expensive things. You love luxury.

Virgo You're careful and methodical, and perhaps one of the hardest workers around. You're very stubborn so you'll achieve your ambitions. Think about working in business or in the medical profession.

Libra Admit it, you can be a bit snooty, can't you? But this is because you're a wonderful idealist who can't imagine life as a down-and-out. You believe that if every-one worked harder, the world would be a better place.

Scorpio You're emotionally intense and can keep a lid on your feelings whatever is happening around you. This makes you strong and single-minded. You're very ambitious and will work your socks off to get to where you want to be.

Sagittarius Although you're a hard worker, you do know when to stop and call it a day. You can be chatty and you're probably very good at foreign languages. Travel should thrill you, especially going abroad and sampling foreign cultures.

Capricorn Surely no-one could work harder than you. You've certainly set your sights to getting to the very top in whatever you want to do, but you also need to ease up now and again. Remember the saying: all work and no play...

Aquarius With your mixture of down-to-earth practi-cality and imaginative ideas, you could certainly go far. In fact, your mind is always twenty paces ahead of everyone else! You may have some odd ideas but just as many brilliant flashes of inspiration.

Pisces You tend to be shy and reserved. Emotionally you're very tender and perhaps you bury yourself in your work in order to hide that sensitivity. You're very kind-hearted, compassionate and brilliant at giving advice. No-one could be as helpful and caring in life as you.

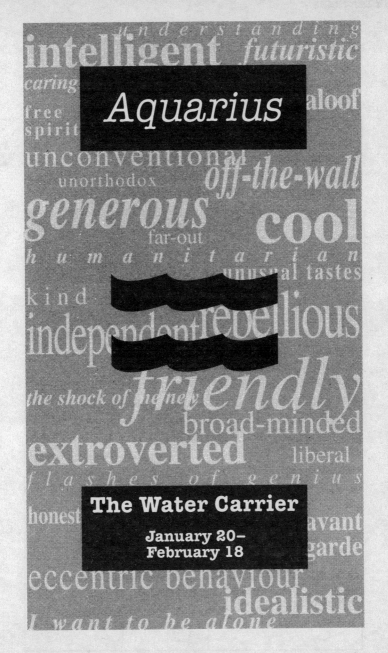

understanding

intelligent futuristic

caring

free
spirit
aloof

Aquarius

unconventional

unorthodox off-the-wall

generous cool

far-out

humanitarian

unusual tastes

kind

independent rebellious

the shock of the new friendly

broad-minded

extroverted liberal

flashes of genius

honest avant garde

The Water Carrier

January 20–
February 18

eccentric behaviour.

idealistic

I want to be alone

Are You A True Aquarian?

Find out how typical you are of your sign. Check only **one** box for each question.

	Often	Sometimes	Never
Do you dress in bright, jazzy or unusual clothes?	◯	◯	◯
Are your ideas more original than your classmates'?	◯	◯	◯
Do you enjoy the company of oddball types of people?	◯	◯	◯
Do you watch sci-fi films, or read sci-fi stories?	◯	◯	◯
Do you like hearing about modern technology or new inventions?	◯	◯	◯
Do you have lots of friends?	◯	◯	◯
Do people find it difficult to understand you?	◯	◯	◯
Do you like to be alone?	◯	◯	◯
When you see people or animals suffering or unhappy, do you want to help them and/or give them some money?	◯	◯	◯

	Often	Sometimes	Never
Do you sometimes think up ways to improve household appliances?	○	○	○
Do you change things around just for the hell of it?	○	○	○
Do you dream about being an astronaut, or of living in outer space?	○	○	○
Do you hate it when people tell you what to do?	○	○	○

Score: You score 2 points for an "Often" answer, 1 point for a "Sometimes" answer, 0 points for a "Never."

0 - 12 You're not a typical Aquarian, so perhaps you were born at the very beginning or at the very end of your sign, which would modify your character. If so, you're what is known as "cuspal" and are a mixture of two signs. If you were born at the very beginning of Aquarius, you share some Capricornian characteristics and should read about that sign as well. If you were born at the end, you share some Piscean characteristics, so read up on that sign too.

13 - 18 Although you do have many Aquarian characteristics, your Moon placement probably modifies your character and personality quite noticeably. Find out more by reading about how the Moon affects your emotions on page 158.

19 and Over You're a true Aquarian. Now read on and find out more about yourself.

Sign Associations

- **Element** – Air
- **Lucky day** – Saturday
- **Lucky number** – 6
- **Stone** – Amethyst
- **Flower** – Snowdrop
- **Color** – Azure blue
- **Aquarius rules** – The legs, shins and ankles

Your Ruling Planet

As an Aquarian, your ruling planet is Uranus so you may be interested in some of the things associated with this planet. The symbol for your ruling planet is:

Uranus is associated with:

- *new inventions, technology, computer sciences*
- *nuclear or atomic energy*
- *electricity and electronics*
- *revolution and sudden change*
- *space exploration*
- *eccentrics*

★ **Famous people who share your sign** ★

Vic Reeves, Michael Hutchence, Oprah Winfrey, Paul Newman, Mark Owen, David Jason, Phil Collins, Mark Owen, Axl Rose, Robbie Williams, Matt Dillon, Michelle Gayle

Keynotes to Aquarius

you belong to the *Air* element, so: you're chatty and sociable. You're also idealistic, particularly about people. Beauty is important to you.

your *talents* and *interests* lie in: scientific subjects, research, technical drawing, social welfare, atomic studies, healing, collecting rare books, teaching, aeronautical engineering, space technology, social work, art, computers, charity work, new inventions.

you *work*: intuitively and inspirationally – often sameness, monotony and the status quo.

you *hate*: sameness, monotony and the status quo (and that doesn't mean the '70s rock group!).

at *school*: you'll like all the camaraderie and bonding with your friends. In class, you're the one who always asks unusual questions and you could spend hours discussing subjects like civil rights or feminism. But it's the science and technological subjects that are more likely to grab your imagination – you know, all that business where they get you to construct a model of something like a heat-seeking missile using only a rubber band, a potato and an old paper cup. You would probably do a good deal better in a modern progressive type of school than in an old-fashioned, traditional sort of environment.

you spend your *money*: either on the sort of gadgets you get from the Science museum or ethnic things from the local New Age shop.

you like your *bedroom* to be: stimulating. So you'll

use vibrant, fluorescent colours to jazz up the atmosphere. If you had a choice you would probably go for ultra modern furniture. But whatever you're stuck with you'll try to make it look different or unusual in some way, either by painting zig-zag stripes across it or doing a cover-up job with posters or stickers.

*you keep **fit** by:* practicing Yoga or T'ai Chi – the more "alternative" the system the better. Sprained ankles can be a problem with people of your sign, so watch out if you're involved in any contact sports.

≋   ≋   ≋

The Aquarian Personality

Aquarians are what's known as progressive thinkers. Those on their wave length will understand them and realize what a truly original turn of mind they possess. Those who aren't, will simply think they're spaced out, weird or plain batty – depending on what generation they belong to!

Of all the signs of the Zodiac, members of this group are perhaps the most broad-minded and tolerant of the lot. They seem able to take on board all sorts of odd human behavior. Tell them about unusual lifestyles or bizarre beliefs and they'll shrug their shoulders and just say, "So what?" "Live and let live" is very definitely the Aquarian motto in life.

You see, Aquarians simply don't get fazed by life's little quirks and eccentricities as other people do. Perhaps it's because being such free spirits themselves they tend to have very different views than the norm. In fact, they hate being "normal." It would bother them to no end if people referred to them as "average" or "ordinary." They like to think of themselves as different, unusual, extraordinary – in every way. They're born with a definite rebellious streak and they simply love saying or doing things that will surprise or shock people.

Although their sign is known as the water-bearer, these people actually belong to the Air element which means that when it comes to emotions, they can be quite cool and breezy. In relationships, it's their head that rules their heart. And yet they can be passionate in many ways: they're passionate about books, latest inventions and new technology. More importantly, they're passionate believers in humanitarian or environmental ideals and they want to make the world a better place.

If you're an Aquarian, are you a person of vision like this?

What you really think about yourself but wouldn't dream of saying to anyone else: *I'm centuries ahead of anyone else.*

What you want most in the world: *To make it a happier place.*

What your mom would say to you: *If you must mess around with your chemistry set, don't you dare set fire to the curtains again!*

What your teacher would write in your school report: *A colorful character.*

What your best friend would say to you: *We're all relying on you to come up with some really wild ideas for the Christmas party this year.*

How to insult a Aquarian: *Oh Gawd! Here comes that hippie weirdo again!*

If your boyfriend is a typical Aquarian...

You can spot him a mile away because he's: attractive in an unusual sort of way. He's tallish, with a broad forehead, prominent cheek-bones and square-cut jaw line. When he flashes that brilliant smile of his at you, it'll make your knees go weak. Though he loves to be ultra-trendy, he won't slavishly follow what everyone else is wearing – he prefers to create his own style. He hasn't much finesse so his shoes may be badly scuffed, for instance, or his jacket could be coming undone at the seam.

- **He likes:** *weird and wonderful things.*

- **He needs:** *some time to himself.*

- **He's great because he's:** *got a good sense of humor.*

- **He's a drag because he's:** *unpredictable.*

- **Never:** *pour cold water on his ideas.*

On your first date with him: you might wonder whether you misunderstood the nature of this date. Are you to take it he invited you round to help him discuss his history project, or is there something more to this relationship? You see, this guy can get so high just talking with you, that he could well forget the romance. It's more like a session at the local debating society than a proper date. Why not suggest you get a couple of pizzas delivered and settle down to a game of truth or dare instead?

On his birthday, spoil him: by taking him to a laser show.

If your girlfriend is a typical Aquarian...

You can spot her a mile away because she's: so different in appearance to everyone else. Her eyes are bright and tilt up at the corners like a cat's. Her skin is terrific and she has masses of hair which she ties up in odd, but somehow stunning, styles. But it's her clothes that really give her away. She'll either be bang up-to-date fashion-wise or way out, even weird, in her dress sense. She doesn't pay a great deal of attention to details but the electric colours she chooses to put together will strike you with cosmic impact!

- **She likes:** *surprises.*

- **She needs:** *her privacy.*

- **She's great because she:** *can be a mind-reader.*

- **She's a drag because she:** *is incredibly meticulous.*

- **Never:** *crush her free spirit.*

On your first date with her: don't be surprised if she's invited the rest of the crowd along too. If she has, you'll be left wondering if this is meant as a brush-off. Take heart, it almost certainly isn't – she's just friendly that way. However, if you don't get on to her wavelength straight away, you're not likely to get another chance. There'll be lots of chat and sooner or later you'll find that she's talking exclusively to you. Then you'll know it's game on.

On her birthday, spoil her: by buying her a computer game.

Aquarius in love

♥ **You have a special understanding with:**
Geminis, Librans and, of course, other Aquarians.

♥ **In a relationship your best qualities are:**
tolerance, understanding, and an ability to be supportive.

♥ **In a relationship your worst qualities are:**
stubborness, a reluctance to talk about your true feelings,
and an inability to trust other people.

♥ **Your ideal partner:** is someone who is clever,
generous and open-minded. Someone with lots of hobbies
so they can keep you interested and on your toes. Someone
who will encourage you to talk about your feelings but
will, at the same time, respect your need for privacy. You
like people who are a bit alternative or way-out. The
boring, the stodgy or the ordinary is definitely not for you.

Dos & don'ts for happy relationships

do ✔	don't ✗
✔ say you're sorry when you're wrong	✗ stress your partner with your urge to be rebellious
✔ learn to trust your partner	✗ lose your sense of humor

Your Aquarius love chart

Aquarius with ♥	Your relationship together ♥ At a glance	
Aries	short-term	♥♥
Taurus	dead end	♥
Gemini	wicked!	♥♥♥♥♥
Cancer	thumbs down	♥
Leo	attraction of opposites?	♥♥♥
Virgo	not a lot in common	♥♥
Libra	ballistic!	♥♥♥♥♥
Scorpio	stressed out	♥
Sagittarius	possible	♥♥♥
Capricorn	no way, José	♥
Aquarius	a winner, but very offbeat	♥♥♥♥♥
Pisces	different needs	♥♥

♥ = grim   ♥♥ = so-so   ♥♥♥ = stick with it

♥♥♥♥ = magnetic   ♥♥♥♥♥ = fwoarrrgh!

The Moon and Your Emotions

Everything you've read about yourself so far has been based on the Sun's position at the time of your birth which, in your case, was in the sign of Aquarius. This tells you a great deal about your character. But if you want to know more about your emotions, you need to know in which sign the Moon was placed when you were born.

Find your Moon sign by turning to the tables on page 187 then read below how it works with your Sun sign to affect and modify your Aquarian nature.

Sun in Aquarius with Moon in:

Aries You're very clever and you catch on really quickly. You're never afraid to be the first to try out something new because doing anything exploratory or controversial gives you a great buzz. You're one of life's true pioneers.

Taurus With this Moon placement you're likely to be solid and stable. You're good at practical subjects and enjoy making things. You may be keen on music and just as good at the Arts as you are in the Sciences, which may make it difficult to decide which subjects to take or which career to choose.

Gemini You're electric. You buzz here, there and everywhere. You juggle so many balls in the air at the same time anyone would think you had ten hands. But you're quick, sharp and highly intelligent. You're a computer whiz-kid.

Cancer Home-loving, caring and kind, despite your breezy Aquarian character you're really quite a softy underneath. You're compassionate and idealistic and may be a big kid all your life so perhaps a career involving children or animals would suit you well. Emotionally, you can sometimes be clingy and then at other times demanding your own independence and space.

Leo The two signs of Leo and Aquarius are both dramatic and flamboyant in their own way, so you can see how doubly colorful a personality you are. Lively, fiery, impulsive and enthusiastic in everything you do, you'll go far.

Virgo The Moon in Virgo gives you a good deal of common sense and practical ability. This combination suggests you're intelligent and that you'll enjoy all forms of research. Try not to spend too long fretting over petty details.

Libra You're everybody's friend! Happy to talk to people all day long, you're sociable and easy-going and much less likely to go against the flow than most other Aquarians would be. Music and the Arts are especially dear to your heart.

Scorpio Though Aquarians normally tend to let their heads rule their hearts, with your Moon in this position, your feelings are deep and powerful – although, of course, you hide this behind a cool and confident mask. You are highly insightful and intuitive.

Sagittarius You can be too impulsive for your own good and now and then prone to putting your foot in it and upsetting people with your tactless remarks. But you have a wonderfully original mind and a truly zany sense of humor.

Capricorn You can be a tireless worker when you get a bee in your bonnet because you're determined to make a success of your life. Perhaps you will find your fame and fortune by turning some of your inventive ideas into practical realities.

Aquarius You have to be a true eccentric – someone so individualistic and unconventional that you go against all the rules simply because they're there. You're wacky and tremendous fun to be with. The term "free spirit" was invented just for you.

Pisces Dreamy and imaginative, your flights of fancy could make you a brilliant artist or writer. If you paint, you'll probably favor the post-modernists or abstract styles. And if you write, you could make it big in fantasy or sci-fi.

Pisces

intuitive
imaginative sensitive
moody
poetic kind
dreamy shy
compassionate
considerate originality
evasive loving
illogical
tender hearted
understandi creative
changea unrealistic
romantic
good sense of humour
temperamental
sympathetic vulnerable
believe love conquers all
musica sulky

The Fish

February 19–
March 20

wishful thinking emotional
impractical
head in the clouds

Are You A True Piscean?

Find out how typical you are of your sign. Check only **one** box for each question.

	Often	Sometimes	Never
Are you good at making up stories?	○	○	○
Do you try not to hurt other people's feelings?	○	○	○
Do you get upset easily?	○	○	○
Are you creative?	○	○	○
Do you think people take advantage of your kind and gentle nature?	○	○	○
Do people pick on you?	○	○	○
Do you find it difficult to make up your mind?	○	○	○
Do your feet bother you in any way?	○	○	○
Do you find you can tune in to other people's feelings?	○	○	○
Are you a bit sneaky (be honest!)?	○	○	○

	Often	Sometimes	Never
Do you keep secrets?	○	○	○
Do you daydream a lot about boyfriends or girlfriends?	○	○	○

Score: You score 2 points for an "Often" answer, 1 point for a "Sometimes" answer, 0 points for a "Never."

0 - 12 You're not a typical Piscean, so perhaps you were born at the very beginning or at the very end of your sign, which would modify your character. If so, you're what is known as "cuspal" and are a mixture of two signs. If you were born at the very beginning of Pisces, you share some Aquarian characteristics and should read about that sign as well. If you were born at the end, you share some of Aries' characteristics, so read up on that sign too.

13 - 18 Although you do have many Piscean characteristics, your Moon placement probably modifies your character and personality quite noticeably. Find out more by reading about how the Moon affects your emotions on page 172.

19 and Over You're a true Piscean. Now read on and find out more about yourself.

Sign Associations

- **Element** – Water
- **Lucky day** – Thursday
- **Lucky number** – 3
- **Stone** – Aquamarine, bloodstone
- **Flower** – Lilac
- **Color** – Sea green
- **Pisces rules** – The feet and the toes

Your Ruling Planet

As a Piscean, your ruling planet is Neptune so you may be interested in some of the things that are associated with this planet. The symbol for Neptune is:

Neptune is associated with:

- *the sea, water, liquids*
- *music*
- *sleep, dream states and confusion*
- *narcotics*
- *chemicals*
- *fishing*
- *the brewing industry*

★ Famous people who share your sign ★

John Leslie, Jon Bon Jovi, Neneh Cherry, Andy Crane, Emilio Estefan, Bruce Willis, Dennis Waterman, Graham Coxton, Rob Lowe, Jasper Carrott, Julie Walters, Prince Edward, Kimberley Davies

Keynotes to Pisces

you belong to the Water element, so: you're sensitive, emotionally intense and your heart often rules your head. You enjoy being near water.

your talents and interests lie in: singing, dancing, playing music, the arts, unusual healing methods, creative use of color, clairvoyance, psychotherapy, the beauty business.

you work: intuitively rather than logically.

you hate: aggression of any sort.

at school: whether you sink or swim under the school system very much depends on the group you're in with. If all your friends are the studious, hard-working kind, then chances are you too will work hard and become fairly academic. If, though, you're in with an idle lot who aren't at all interested in doing well at school, then you're likely to cop out too. In general, though, you'll prefer the Arts subjects to the Sciences. At the least hint of any emotional trouble, either between you and your friends or you and your teachers, you'd make any excuse to stay at home rather than go in and face the music.

you spend your money: on tapes and CDs, on posters of your fave pop group and on buying little gifts for other people.

you like your bedroom to be: soft and romantic. It must be airy and light because a dark and somber place immediately plonks you into a sad mood. So you'll use lots of white with perhaps hints of greens, blues and purples or mauve to remind you of the shimmering waters of the sea.

you keep fit by: dreaming that you're a sports champ. In truth, you're not really built to withstand any rough and tumble type of physical activity so contact sports are really not your scene at all. However, you do have rhythm – lots of it – so you should do well in gymnastics, but you particularly excel at swimming and, especially, at ballet. Yoga, or a gentle stroll along the river-bank or by the sea, would be helpful when you're upset or stressed out.

The Piscean Personality

Pisceans are just about the kindest, gentlest and most tender-hearted people one is ever likely to meet. They're dreamy romantics, terrifically imaginative and they often excel in painting and writing. And because they're also sensitive and receptive to vibes, it means they can pick up rhythm and beat really easily so many become brilliant musicians, dancers, poets – and even cat-walk models too!

Belonging to the Water element means that Pisceans are ruled by emotion. Feelings play a huge part in their lives. For a start, they seem to intuitively feel their way along rather than rationally working things out. And secondly, they're also able to tune in to other people's feelings too. It's like a double whammy of feelings – they live their own and other people's emotions at the same time. For instance, if someone is sad and unhappy, then the Piscean will instantly become sad and unhappy too. If someone in their company is happy and cheerful, the Piscean's mood will automatically respond by cheering up and becoming happy as well. If someone is unhappy, no-one will understand that pain more acutely than his/her Piscean friend.

But this ability to empathise can also make Pisceans vulnerable because, in taking on other people's emotions and moods, they can be easily led. And because they're so trusting, they can also be taken for a ride.

Tender, loving and affectionate, Pisceans are the world's greatest pacifists. They abhor violence so much that even the tiniest bit of aggression will make them physically ill.

If you're a Piscean, do you think this sounds like you?

What you really think about yourself but wouldn't dream of saying to anyone else: *I'm so afraid no-one will like me.*

What you want most in the world: *To make it a beautiful place.*

What your mom would say to you: *Stop mooning about and get a move on or you'll be late for school!*

What your teacher would write in your school report: *Strong tendency to daydream.*

What your best friend would say to you: *Here, you're good at poems. Why don't you make one up for the teacher's retirement party?*

How to insult a Piscean: *Get real, you fish-faced dweeb!*

If your boyfriend is a typical Piscean...

You can spot him a mile away because he's: cuddly and cute and when he catches your eye and smiles at you you'll see those irresistibly kissable dimples in his cheeks. There's a soft and tender expression in his eyes and a sort of "please-be-gentle-with-me" look about him that makes you want to take him home with you and look after him. He'll be wearing loose, comfortable clothes – he hates anything tight and starchy – and he looks terrific in turquoise blue.

- **He likes:** *poetry.*

- **He needs:** *to make the most of his talents.*

- **He's great because he's:** *fabulously gentle.*

- **He's a drag because he's:** *so gullible he'll swallow any old sob story anyone tells him.*

- **Never:** *hurt his feelings.*

On your first date with him: he'll be terribly anxious that nothing goes wrong, and half the battle will be getting a smile out of him. After that it's all plain sailing because he's so kind and gentle and very spiritual. You'll find him knowledgeable, especially about music and artistic things. He's highly sentimental and will probably want to do something yummily romantic like sitting side-by-side in the park and watching the sunset. Or perhaps you'll walk barefoot, arm-in-arm, across the dew-dampened grass. It's what he calls "sharing a deep mystical experience" with you.

On his birthday, spoil him: by giving him a beautiful book on watercolor painting.

If your girlfriend is a typical Piscean...

You can spot her a mile away because she's: a real turn-on. She's sweet and soft and ever so sexy. Perhaps it's those lovely soft eyes with their far-away dreamy look, or her fine hair and delicate complexion, that makes her appear so fragile that you want to hold her tight and protect her from harm. She won't be wearing anything crisp or sharp because she likes soft, flowing, feminine clothes in sugar-candy shades of green, blue, lilac or pink.

- **She likes:** *looking after children and caring for the environment.*

- **She needs:** *loads of support.*

- **She's great because she's:** *understanding and sympathetic.*

- **She's a drag because she's:** *very clingy.*

- **Never:** *be cruel to her.*

On your first date with her: don't be surprised if she's a bit nervous or apprehensive to begin with. Pisceans tend to be a bit wary of people they don't know and they need time to learn to trust you. Make her smile, make her laugh, and soon you'll find you're talking about all sorts of things. She's so understanding and such a brilliant listener that you'll be pouring out your troubles to her, telling her about your dreams and desires and even confessing your most intimate secrets to her. She'll snuggle up to you as you wrap your arms around her in her all-time favorite bear hug.

On her birthday, spoil her: by taking her to the ballet.

Pisces in love

♥ **You have a special understanding with:**
Cancerians, Scorpios and, of course, other Pisceans.

♥ **In a relationship your best qualities are:**
unselfishness, you're a great listener, very adaptable and
you can create a magical environment for your partner
wherever you go.

♥ **In a relationship your worst qualities are:**
you're dependent, insecure and you need your confidence
boosted all the time.

♥ **Your ideal partner:** has to be someone who is
romantic and who sweeps you off your feet. You need
someone who is gentle and understanding and who won't
put you down, but at the same time who is strong and
supportive, and a calming, reassuring influence on your
turbulent emotions. Above all, it must be someone who can
make you laugh.

Dos & don'ts for happy relationships

do ✔	don't ✗
✔ stand on your own two feet	✗ suffer in silence
✔ own up to your own and your partner's faults	✗ cling on to a relationship that's passed its sell-by date

Your Pisces love chart

Pisces with ♥	Your relationship together ♥	At a glance
Aries	many spills but few thrills	♥
Taurus	tender but not electric	♥♥♥
Gemini	can be irritating	♥♥
Cancer	smoochy woochy!	♥♥♥♥♥
Leo	steamy	♥♥♥
Virgo	attraction of opposites?	♥♥♥
Libra	so refined	♥♥♥♥
Scorpio	smoldering	♥♥♥♥♥
Sagittarius	mis-match	♥
Capricorn	not much going for it	♥♥
Aquarius	spiritual, if nothing else	♥♥
Pisces	dreamy	♥♥♥♥♥

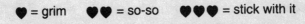

♥ = grim   ♥♥ = so-so   ♥♥♥ = stick with it

♥♥♥♥ = magnetic   ♥♥♥♥♥ = fwoarrrgh!

The Moon and Your Emotions

Everything you've read about yourself so far has been based on the Sun's position at the time of your birth which, in your case, was in the sign of Pisces. This tells you a great deal about your character. But if you want to know more about your emotions, you need to know in which sign the Moon was placed when you were born.

Find your Moon sign by turning to the tables on page 187 then read below how it works with your Sun sign to affect and modify your Piscean nature.

Sun in Pisces with Moon in:

Aries More independent and assertive than most other Pisceans, you're dreamy and romantic but also brave and determined. You're energetic and resilient and able to snap out of sulky moods fairly quickly.

Taurus The Moon in this Earthy sign will help to stabilize your emotions and will keep your feelings on a more even keel. You're likely to be extremely imaginative and very creative. Brilliant at painting, music and writing.

Gemini You're chatty and fun-loving and you can come up with the most imaginative stories ever. You could make your fortune one day by writing romantic fiction. The snag is you can be a bit of a butterfly and tend not to see things through.

Cancer A lovely and loving homebody, with a flair for creative domestic pursuits, such as cooking and sewing, for example. You're very sensitive and understanding towards others and would make a brilliant nurse.

Leo In your rich imagination you dream about romance and fantasize about a life of wealth, luxury and elegance. In real life, you're talented and creative and you really could achieve some of those things if you believe in yourself and in your abilities.

Virgo You're extremely perceptive and able to read people like a book. You enjoy detailed work but perhaps spend so long worrying over little niggly points, that you give yourself more problems than really exist. Sciences as well as Arts appeal to you.

Libra You have a great sense of beauty and elegance and anything gross makes you want to escape into a romantic fantasy. Working with others would help you achieve a good deal more in life than working on your own.

Scorpio You're gifted with deep psychological insight and you could become a fine doctor or exceptional pyschoanalyst one day if you were to apply yourself. You're sexy but a tad prone to becoming too intense in your relationships.

Sagittarius A Water Sun combined with a Fire Moon can make you racy and ever so steamy. You're likely to be a lot more independent than most other Pisceans and interested in travel and foreign cultures.

Capricorn Perhaps the hardest worker amongst all the Piscean combinations, which should enable you to achieve your ambitions and get to the top of your chosen field. Don't let worry or a lack of self-confidence scupper your chances.

Aquarius You're one of life's givers: caring, committed to humanitarian causes and to helping others. With this Air

Moon you are able to work your moods out rationally. You have some pretty advanced ideas and may appear a bit eccentric at times.

Pisces You're highly emotional and sensitive and should apply your amazing imaginative and creative powers to painting and writing. You'd wow everyone as a dancer or skater, or, with your Water Sun and Moon, maybe you should take up synchronized swimming?

Your Star Sign Parents (and how to handle them!)

What sort of a relationship do you have with your mom and dad – easy, difficult? Do you think they understand you, or are you always falling out? And do they give you a hard time when you want to stay out late or when you've set your heart on spending all your savings on something they don't approve of?

Well, they may be your parents but they're people too and that means they belong to a Star Sign just like you. If you get on with them like a house on fire, it might be because they belong to the same sign as you. Or perhaps their sign belongs to the same element group.

This is how the signs are grouped together:

Earth	Air	Fire	Water
Taurus	Gemini	Aries	Cancer
Virgo	Libra	Leo	Scorpio
Capricorn	Aquarius	Sagittarius	Pisces

In general, people belonging to the same group tend to see and feel things in the same way. They behave in similar ways and like the same kinds of things.

But if you don't belong to the same groupings, it doesn't mean you won't see eye-to-eye with your mom, or that you're bound to get a tough time from your dad. It might mean, though, that understanding each other requires just a little bit more work.

It might just help, however, to get some insights into the way your parents tick by reading up about them under their birth signs. For all you know, you might also pick up some valuable tips on how to get the best out of them.

So, if you want the low-down, check out their signs now.

Aries (March 21–April 19)

If your mom's an Aries: she'll want to know where you've been, who you've been with, what you said, what they said, what you did next . . . get the picture? It's not so much that she's nosy (well, all right, she is a bit), it's more that she just wants to be involved. And involve herself she will – she'll join the parent/teacher committee, she'll sign up for karate lessons with you, she'll cheer the loudest at your sports day, she'll take you to that pop concert – and enjoy it too! Cooking and cleaning aren't really her strong points, but there's one thing you can rely on – your Aries mom will always be behind you.

If your dad's an Aries: He could be a fitness freak. He'll have boundless energy and you'll have to work hard to keep up with him. No, it's no use trying to wriggle out of it, he'll expect you there right alongside him. If he can't keep up, he'll want to know the reason why. And when you do try to explain that you're worn out, or even – heaven forbid! – that you simply don't like all this physical stuff, he may lack sensitivity towards your problem. Well, you know how impatient he is! Under other circumstances, though, he'd stand by you and defend you to the hilt. If you want to get into his good books, or even bond with him, take him camping, or fishing, or to a football game. Even better, take up a sport you like – that should do the trick.

Taurus (April 20–May 20)

If your mom's a Taurean: you'll be loved, cuddled and thoroughly spoiled. Taureans make lovely, caring moms and if anyone should try to harm a hair on your precious head, they'll have one heck of an angry raging bull to deal with! Mind you, she'll expect you to keep your room tidy. This mom won't take kindly to being hassled. If you want to bring a friend home for dinner or stay out later than normal, it's no good springing it on her at the last minute – she'll just get disgruntled. But give her plenty of warning, slowly and subtly get her used to the idea and, if you can, give her a practical reason for whatever it is you want to do – catching the earlier bus means you'd have to change at least twice but the later one drops you right outside your door, for example – then she'll more than likely agree to your terms. Just remember those key words: safety and security. Reassure her about that and you've got it made.

If your dad's a Taurean: you'll be loved and protected. Perhaps over-protected – perhaps wrapped from head to toe in cotton-wool. He can be strict and a bit old-fashioned but he really does have your best interests at heart. If you're defiant or lock horns with him, you'll just bring out his stubborn streak and he'll simply dig his hooves in. But you can wind him round your little finger with a bit of charm and a lot of affection (he's no fool, he'll know exactly where you're coming from, but it'll work like a dream anyway). You could try a bit of 'money logic' – explain that whatever it is you want to buy would be an investment, or is better value than something else.

Gemini (May 21–June 20)

If your mom's a Gemini: she's not a mommy type of mom at all, more like a friend than a mother really. And because she looks so young, people think she's your big sister anyway. She might be away from home more than most parents, because of her hobbies or her work, but when she comes home she'll love chattering away and sharing the gossip she's picked up on her travels. When you're feeling blue she knows exactly how to lift your spirits with a funny story or a joke. By the way, never try to pull the wool over her eyes – she's far too sharp and far too quick. It'll be much better to lay your cards on the table and give her a set of logical reasons for whatever it is you want.

If your dad's a Gemini: he may not be around a lot because he's traveling or working away from home, or out pursuing one or other of his many interests. But when he is around he'll love talking to you. You'll find him very entertaining, always full of stories and jokes. He's a bit of a Peter Pan type and never seems to grow old (or perhaps grow up!). Because of that you don't feel there's a generation gap between you. You can't hoodwink him so don't even try. And it's debatable whether you could appeal to his emotions either. What you can do, though, is remember that he's clever and inventive – you could try to play him at his own game (he likes a good story). But by far the best policy with this dad is to talk to him honestly. He'll respect the grown-up approach and give you a good hearing.

Cancer (June 21–July 22)

If your mom's a Cancerian: she's a real old-fashioned type of mom, always spoiling you with love and attention, fussing over you to make sure you've got your warm sweater on or telling you to do up your coat before you go out. Cuddling is her favorite hobby, so if you're the sort who doesn't appreciate being smothered in kisses you'd better not get within arm's length of her. She loves cooking – especially exotic recipes she's found in a magazine. Of course, this means there's always something tasty in the fridge for when you come home from school. She'll take whatever job she does very seriously and work hard. Getting around a Cancerian mom is easy as pie – just give her a great big bear hug and she's putty in your hands.

If your dad's a Cancerian: he loves having kids around so he won't complain when you want to bring the gang back to your house. He'll even miss his favorite program to drive them all home again afterward. At other times, though, he can be stern and crabby – but this is usually after a long, tiring day, and anyway, you recognize the signs by now and know to keep out of his way when he's feeling like that. When you want something from your Cancerian dad, forget the heavy pressure tactics. If you come on too heavy and too strong, he'll simply clam up. The best way to get round him is to get him all nostalgic. Talk about his childhood a bit, what he calls the "good old days," and ask him what it was like when he was growing up. Commiserate with him about how different things are these days. Appealing to his emotions like this should get him just where you want him.

Leo (July 23–August 22)

If your mom's a Leo: she'll love you heaps but she'll expect you to love her heaps in return. She'll teach you good manners and bring you up to be well-behaved and respectful to your elders. She'll demand high standards in your appearance, in your work and behavior. Whatever you do, don't embarrass her in public. The way to get your mom eating out of your hand is to tell her she's the best mom in the world often, very, very often. Flattery will get you everywhere with this dame. Also, whatever it is you want her to agree to, make it sound like fun. And she's pretty generous with things like pocket money. She's a fun-loving creature and will want her little cubs to have as much fun in their lives as she has in hers.

  If your dad's a Leo: he'll probably spoil you in lots of ways – like a Leo mom, he's a generous soul. You'll have to put up with his bossiness, though. Well, you know how he's always telling you how to do things, and how not to do things, and how he's positive his way's the best. Now, this dad is playful but when the chips are down, he demands respect and loyalty and there'll be no end of trouble if you don't comply. He'll also want to see you working hard, being happy and successful. Don't forget, you're his creation so he's bound to be proud of you anyway, and that's half the battle already. Keep on your dad's good side by giving him praise – little and often. But when you want something special, explain what a challenge it will be for you and how pleased he'll be with you afterwards for having succeeded, scored, achieved or whatever. He's bound to fall for that one!

Virgo (August 23–September 22)

If your mom's a Virgo: she's lovely and practical and down-to-earth. Always busy and bustling, she's fiercely houseproud and has a thing about hygiene. If your standards of tidiness aren't quite as high as hers, you'll be forever in hot water – literally as well as metaphorically. Whatever you do, don't arrive at the table with grubby hands and especially not if you need to get on her good side. If there's going to be a battle field in your home, it's likely to center around your room – especially if you're the sort of person who thinks a little bit of mess simply makes a place look more homely and comfortable! Perhaps you could come to an arrangement – something like, if she makes some concessions about the state of your bedroom, you promise to clean it every week, or every time granny comes to stay, or that sort of thing. Do remember that Virgo moms are worriers. She'll worry about you, about your progress, how you're doing at school, who your friends are, what the neighbors are going to say about your latest hair style, etc., etc. This is her way of caring for you and what she needs is loads and loads of reassurance and masses of cuddles to show you understand her and to bring out that squidgy soft center she has inside.

If your dad's a Virgo: you'll know just what a hard-worker he is. He'll expect you to work hard as well and if you don't, he'll want to know the reason why. If you bring home a school report that has "diligent" or "industrious" or even "tries hard" written all over it, he'll be well-pleased. But if it says "easily distracted" or "disappointing results" or that dreaded "could do better," then beware as sparks will inevitably fly! Being ruled by Mercury means that your Virgo dad is clever at maths, so don't try to pull the wool over his eyes about pocket money or about the cost of living. When you want something it's no use appealing to his emotions, that just won't wash where a Virgo's concerned. You stand a much better chance of getting somewhere if you appeal to his logic and common sense. And because he's dead sharp over itsy-bitsy details, for heaven's sake get your facts straight – if you slip up you'll be caught.

Libra (September 23–October 22)

If your mom's a Libran: she'll want you to look beautiful so she'll buy you lovely clothes and teach you that quality is better than quantity. She's scrupulously fair, and she'll go to great pains to make sure that you and your brothers and sisters are treated the same. For example, if there's chocolate cake for a snack she'll insist you all get exactly the same amount – not a crumb less, not a crumb more. When you need to wheedle something out of this mom, wait for a calm moment. Then, when you ask her for whatever it is you want, make sure you use the words: it's only fair. That's her weak spot, you see. Trigger her sense of justice and you'll have her eating out of your hand.

If your dad's a Libran: you probably get on with him better now that you're grown up than when you were a sticky, pukey child leaving chocolate fingerprints everywhere. He believes in sensible discussions so he'll enjoy having lots of intelligent conversations with you. This dad is quite easy to handle as long as you're reasonable. You'll known by now he's terrible at making up his mind and often will put off a decision so as not to upset you by saying "no" there and then. He can't abide arguments so he may simply give in to your requests. Present your case to him intelligently and you can be sure this dad will give you a very fair hearing.

Scorpio (October 23–November 21)

If your mom's a Scorpio: you'll know that she's totally devoted to you. She could be unusual – perhaps gorgeous-looking or dramatically mysterious. Whatever it is, there's something rather exciting about her. There'll be times when she's impatient – especially if she's trying to teach you something and all you want to do is lark around. Then she'll lose her cool and come down on you like a ton of bricks. But if you work hard and apply yourself, you won't find a more encouraging mom anywhere. Handling this mom requires a good bit of subtlety. Cross her at your own risk! Just remember that you won't win against her in a head-on confrontation, so don't even try. Learn to cut your losses or take the consequences.

   If your dad's a Scorpio: he's probably quite strict and a bit of a mystery to you sometimes. He has high standards and expects you to go by the rules. But he's extremely protective and the sort of guy you'll want to look up to. You'd have to get up ever so early in the morning to get the better of this dad, and even then it's debatable whether you'd get what you wanted. Essentially, he's got a suspicious mind so he'll see you coming a mile off. Put your case by showing him it's all legit and above board, make your argument one hundred per cent water-tight and persist with steady but gentle pressure. But you've got to get the pressure just right here, and only experience will show you how much and for how long will do the trick. Never, never abuse his trust in you or go beyond your agreement – you won't get a second chance. Oh, and by the way, learn to quit while you're ahead.

Sagittarius (November 22–December 21)

If your mom's a Sagittarian: you'll find she's a happy-go-lucky type and probably won't mind too much if your bedroom floor is littered with dirty clothes. But she will mind very much if you're narrow-minded and unkind to others. She'll love reading you stories – the house is probably chock-full of books. If she didn't go to university when she was younger, this mom might be studying for a degree right now. Move over, she needs half the dining room table to do her homework on it, too, you know. Sagittarian moms won't enjoy the role of housewife, so at meal-times she'll like to think of cooking and eating as hugely social affairs with everyone pitching in, talking, laughing and doing their bit together. Or else she might suggest a routine where each of you gets to cook and clean up in turn – at least you'll learn how to look after yourself. Handling your Sagittarian mom is easy, really. Tell her that whatever it is you want to do will broaden your mind and help you develop your independence.

If your dad's a Sagittarian: he passionately believes in education and broadening one's horizons, so he'll be especially pleased every time you get good grades and even happier if you decide to go into higher ed. When he takes you out, which he loves to do, he's always pointing things out and you may sometimes feel you're constantly under instruction. But if you listen to him, you're likely to learn quite a bit. To get the best out of this dad, paint him the picture of what you want on a wide canvass. Explain what your ultimate objective is but please spare him the itsy-bitsy details, otherwise his eyes will glaze over and you'll lose his interest altogether. Be as positive and optimistic of the outcome as you can – Sagittarians are suckers for optimism – and if you can put the request in a witty way, or throw in a joke here or there, even better.

Capricorn (December 22–January 19)

If your mom's a Capricorn: she could be a successful businesswoman as well as a super-efficient mom. You'll never need to say, "Mom, I can't find a clean shirt," because it, like all the rest of your clothes, is likely to be all nicely pressed and hanging up in your wardrobe. In the Capricorn household, there's a place for everything and everything's in its place. The freezer, too, is probably well stocked with food. Your Capricorn mom is likely to be a busy beaver so you'll need to get her to sit down and relax a bit. Tell her to stop worrying about her work, about the cat or about the lawn that needs mowing. Sit her down and gently massage her aching feet. Tell her you think she's great and that you really appreciate all the work she does for you. She may reply with a rather dry remark – but at least you'll know you've got her just where you want her.

If your dad's a Capricorn: you won't need reminding that this is one tough cookie. For a start, he tends to be a workaholic and probably expects you to be one too. He's likely to be fairly strict and will treat you like a grown-up – but then he'll expect you to act like one too! He'll want to see you working hard and getting good marks at school – and if you don't he'll think it's because you're not trying hard enough. This dad will be ambitious for you because success is very important to him. So, as long as he sees you making good progress, you'll be winning. You may not be able to wind this Billy Goat Gruff round your little finger, but you could probably get what you want by appealing to the snobby side of his nature. If there's something you're after, tell him how much better it will make you appear, or what an achievement it would be. Make your arguments as practical as possible. Be calm but persistent and remember your parent belongs to the Earth element. Let your motto be: it's the steady drip that wears away the stone.

Aquarius (January 20–February 18)

If your mom's an Aquarian: she'll expect you to get on with things on your own, to experiment for yourself and find out how things are done. She likes to give you your own space and your own time and will be thrilled when you come up with your own solutions to things – no matter how bizarre they may be. She's a great campaigner and probably belongs to all sorts of groups. She's unconventional to say the least and often does weird things, like suddenly springing a surprise picnic in the middle of winter, or deciding to change the furniture around ten minutes before bedtime. Twisting this odd-ball around your little finger may require some ingenuity on your part since she'll probably see right through you anyway. With an Aquarian mom, honesty is, far and away, your best policy.

If your dad's an Aquarian: he's got some pretty advanced ideas about kids, about education, about politics, about life – well, about everything, really. He's never fazed by people's behavior and thinks the extraordinary is the ordinary, so he's unlikely to be shocked by anything you get into. In fact, it'll probably be the other way around – you'll be shocked by his behavior! He's likely to be a bit of an inventor too, so you'll be tripping over lots of electronic bits and pieces around the house. You learn from an early age to expect the unexpected. The more original your request, the better your chances of getting what you want. Don't bombard him, he won't like that. If you can persuade him that what you want will result in you being a better, wiser, kinder person, or even that it will help humanity at large, then you're in with a chance. Don't despair if he looks as if he's going to refuse at first. Hang around a bit, because he may suddenly spin around and grant you everything you've asked for. You see, you simply can't tell what an Aquarian parent will do next!

Pisces (February 19–March 20)

If your mom's a Piscean: you'll know she's soft and tender and very, very loving. Whatever she does, she always puts her children first, so you can be assured that she'll be there for you, ready to give you advice, and teach you to be kind and good. She's really gentle and very kind to everybody and everything. You'll probably have loads of pets because she can't help taking in strays. Whether man or beast, if it's wounded, hungry or unloved, she'll nurse it back to health and happiness. When you were little she'll have protected and nurtured you with masses of TLC. Now as you grow older, you'll feel it's you who has to protect and nurture her instead. There's no real discipline in a Piscean mom's household, so as long as you're not being unkind, you'll probably find life an easy ride.

If your dad's a Piscean: you'll know that he's devoted to you, to your brothers and sisters, to your mom, to the cat and the dog and even to the goldfish if you have one. There's very little in this world that would make your dad get into a fight – unless you or any of his loved ones were threatened. Then he would probably go so far as to lay down his life for you – that's how much this guy feels for you. But altruism apart, life with a Piscean dad means very few rules, which has obvious good points but a down-side too. This easy-going dad can dither about, unable to steer you in a firm direction or make a concrete decision. He will, though, listen to your point of view and probably go along with you so as not to upset you. Ultimately, he'll bend over backwards to please you, so never do anything underhand where he's concerned and never, ever, take advantage of this man's kind nature.

Moon Signs))●

The charts in this section will help you find out which sign the Moon was in at the time you were born.

It takes the Moon about two and a half days to travel through each sign of the Zodiac, and the only way to find out its exact position at the very moment of your birth is to consult what's called an "astrological ephemeris." This contains pages and pages of tables and takes time and practice to get accurate results. However, it is possible to take a short cut . . .

The three boxes in this section contain all the information you need to work out your own Moon Sign.

Box 1 shows the Moon's position on the first day of each month for the years from 1920 right through into the next century.
Box 2 contains the days of the month and shows the number of signs the Moon travels through in her monthly orbit across the heavens.
Box 3 contains a wheel listing the signs of the Zodiac in sequence.

How to find your Moon Sign

First, find the year in which you were born in the left-hand columns of box 1. Now, run your finger along the line until you reach the column of your birth month. This will show the sign the Moon was in on the first day of that month. We'll call this the starter sign.

Next, turn to box 2 and look for the day of the month on which you were born. The number underneath each date shows how many signs the Moon has travelled through since the first of the month. Add this number of signs to the starter sign. Box 3 makes this easy for you – simply put your finger on your starter sign in the wheel and count through however many signs you need in an anti-clockwise direction.

Here are a couple of examples to show how it's done.

Sophie was born on August 30, 1980.
From box 1 find 1980.
Run your finger along the row to the column headed August.
On 1 August the Moon was in Aries. Aries is the starter sign.
From box 2 find the 30th.
Next to the 30th is the number 1, which shows that one sign has to be added on to the starter sign.

Find the starter sign, which in Sophie's case is Aries, in box 3.
Adding one sign to Aries gives you Taurus.

Sophie's Moon Sign is Taurus.

Let's try with someone else. Damon Albarn was born on March 23, 1968.

From box 1 find 1968.
Run your finger along the row to the column headed March.
On 1 March the Moon was in Pisces. Pisces is the starter sign.
From box 2 find the 23rd.
Next to the 23rd is the number 10, which shows that 10 signs have to be added on to the starter sign.

Find the starter sign, which in Damon's case is Pisces, in box 3.
Adding ten signs to Pisces gives you Capricorn.

Damon's Moon Sign is Capricorn.

Box 1: Moon Signs on First Day of each Month

Year of Birth					JAN	FEB	MAR	APR	MAY	JUN	JUL	AUG	SEP	OCT	NOV	DEC
1920	1939	1958	1977	1996	TAU	GEM	CAN	VIR	LIB	SAG	CAP	AQU	ARI	TAU	CAN	LEO
1921	1940	1959	1978	1997	LIB	SCO	SAG	CAP	AQU	ARI	TAU	CAN	LEO	VIR	SCO	SAG
1922	1941	1960	1979	1998	AQU	ARI	ARI	GEM	CAN	LEO	VIR	SCO	CAP	AQU	ARI	TAU
1923	1942	1961	1980	1999	GEM	LEO	LEO	LIB	SCO	CAP	AQU	ARI	TAU	GEM	LEO	VIR
1924	1943	1962	1981	2000	LIB	SAG	CAP	AQU	ARI	TAU	GEM	LEO	LIB	SCO	SAG	CAP
1925	1944	1963	1982	2001	PIS	TAU	TAU	CAN	LEO	LIB	SCO	SAG	AQU	PIS	TAU	GEM
1926	1945	1964	1983	2002	LEO	VIR	LIB	SCO	SAG	AQU	PIS	TAU	CAN	LEO	VIR	LIB
1927	1946	1965	1984	2003	SAG	CAP	AQU	PIS	TAU	GEM	LEO	VIR	SCO	SAG	AQU	PIS
1928	1947	1966	1985	2004	ARI	GEM	GEM	LEO	VIR	SCO	SAG	AQU	PIS	ARI	GEM	CAN
1929	1948	1967	1986	2005	VIR	SCO	SCO	CAP	AQU	PIS	TAU	GEM	LEO	VIR	LIB	SAG
1930	1949	1968	1987	2006	CAP	PIS	PIS	TAU	GEM	LEO	VIR	SCO	SAG	CAP	PIS	ARI
1931	1950	1969	1988	2007	TAU	CAN	CAN	VIR	LIB	SAG	CAP	PIS	ARI	GEM	CAN	LEO
1932	1951	1970	1989	2008	LIB	SAG	SAG	AQU	PIS	TAU	GEM	CAN	VIR	LIB	SAG	CAP
1933	1952	1971	1990	2009	PIS	ARI	TAU	GEM	CAN	VIR	LIB	SAG	CAP	AQU	ARI	TAU
1934	1953	1972	1991	2010	CAN	VIR	VIR	LIB	SAG	CAP	PIS	ARI	GEM	CAN	VIR	LIB
1935	1954	1973	1992	2011	SCO	CAP	CAP	PIS	ARI	GEM	CAN	VIR	SCO	SAG	CAP	AQU
1936	1955	1974	1993	2012	ARI	TAU	GEM	LEO	VIR	LIB	SCO	CAP	PIS	ARI	TAU	CAN
1937	1956	1975	1994	2013	LEO	LIB	LIB	SAG	CAP	PIS	ARI	TAU	CAN	LEO	LIB	SCO
1938	1957	1976	1995	2014	CAP	AQU	PIS	ARI	TAU	CAN	LEO	LIB	SCO	CAP	AQU	ARI

Box 2: Number of Signs to be added for each day of the Month

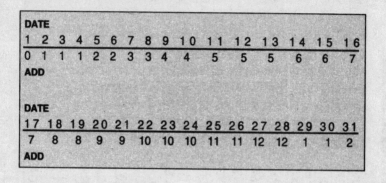

DATE															
1	2	3	4	5	6	7	8	9	10	11	12	13	14	15	16
0	1	1	1	2	2	3	3	4	4	5	5	5	6	6	7
ADD															

DATE														
17	18	19	20	21	22	23	24	25	26	27	28	29	30	31
7	8	8	9	9	10	10	10	11	11	12	12	1	1	2
ADD														

Box 3:

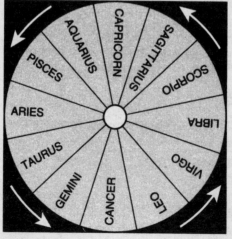

The sign which the Moon was in at the time of your birth tells you a lot about your feelings, how you handle your emotions, and how you behave within your relationships.

Here is a quick break-down of how you handle your emotions and feelings according to which sign your Moon is in. However, in order to get a wider picture, it's important to see how your Moon Sign interacts with your Sun Sign. When you have read the keynotes below, go back to your own Sun Sign chapter to find out more.

Remember, though, that if you were born very early in the morning or late at night, this way of finding your Moon Sign may not be accurate. If you don't think your Moon Sign describes you very well, look at the sign just before or the one just after.

Keynotes to your emotions

Moon in:

Aries Short temper, changeable moods, sometimes emotionally over-the-top. Independent, impulsive, competitive. You need to be in charge, and can conflict with Dad if he's too strict.

Taurus Emotionally steady, solid and reliable. You tend to be possessive, but you are emotionally mature and get on well with older people.

Gemini Easily bored, and may flit from one friend to another. Brilliant at controlling your feelings and working out your emotions. You get on with everybody.

Cancer Emotionally instinctive and intuitive. You are able to tap into other people's feelings, so you're easily influenced by other people's moods. You're very close to your mother.

Leo Warm, generous and loving. Emotionally dramatic, you tend to exaggerate your feelings. The need to be praised means you do things to please others.

Virgo Emotionally shy, you keep your feelings to yourself. You show your affection for others by doing things for them rather than telling them how you feel.

Libra You're emotionally easygoing and laid back. You're very good at making and keeping friends. Quarreling upsets you deeply. You like everything and everybody to be nice.

Scorpio Emotionally, you're deep, deep, deep! But you don't show your feelings on the surface, so others see you as a bit mysterious. Beware jealousy and taking yourself too seriously.

Sagittarius Warm and easy-going. You're open, honest and frank about your own feelings, so you find it hard to accept that some people aren't. You hate being tied down.

Capricorn You can appear emotionally cool but that's because you take a serious and mature attitude to relationships. You relate best to older people.

Aquarius You're tolerant, open-minded and unconventional in your views about relationships, and excellent at working out your own and other people's problems. The whole world is your friend.

Pisces You're emotionally ultra-sensitive, which means you get hurt easily. You're kind, considerate, tender-hearted and understanding. Family rows literally make you feel ill.